THE ARCHAEOLOGY
OF THE
ANGLO-SAXON
SETTLEMENTS

BY

E. THURLOW LEEDS

With an Introduction

by

J. N. L. MYRES

OXFORD

AT THE CLARENDON PRESS

Oxford University Press, Ely House, London W. 1

GLASGOW   NEW YORK   TORONTO   MELBOURNE   WELLINGTON
CAPE TOWN   SALISBURY   IBADAN   NAIROBI   DAR ES SALAAM   LUSAKA   ADDIS ABABA
BOMBAY   CALCUTTA   MADRAS   KARACHI   LAHORE   DACCA
KUALA LUMPUR   SINGAPORE   HONG KONG   TOKYO

FIRST PUBLISHED 1913
REPRINTED LITHOGRAPHICALLY IN GREAT BRITAIN
AT THE UNIVERSITY PRESS, OXFORD
BY VIVIAN RIDLER
PRINTER TO THE UNIVERSITY
1970

INTRODUCTION TO 1970 REPRINT

It is now generally recognized that, by his publication in 1913 of *The Archaeology of the Anglo-Saxon Settlements*, E. T. Leeds,[1] then Assistant Keeper in the Department of Antiquities of the Ashmolean Museum, laid the foundations for the modern study of Anglo-Saxon antiquities and established their importance for a proper understanding of the early history of this country. It was in every sense a pioneer work, and, while subsequent discoveries and interpretations, mostly based in the first place on Leeds's own stimulating ideas, have modified many of his conclusions, it remains the basis on which all subsequent studies in early Anglo-Saxon archaeology have been built. It is indeed still an indispensable tool for all who interest themselves in this subject, and its reprinting will be welcomed for enabling a gap to be filled in the working libraries of many students and scholars both here and abroad.

At the time when it was written there was no general account of Anglo-Saxon archaeology in print, except the Baron De Baye's *Industrie Anglo-Saxonne*, available in English as *The Industrial Arts of the Anglo-Saxons* (1893), and rightly described by Leeds (p. 3) as 'a somewhat antiquated work and not always correct'. The wide survey by G. Baldwin Brown (*The Arts in Early England*, iii and iv)

---

[1] The fullest account of the author's life, and the best appreciation of his place in archaeological scholarship, is in *Dark-Age Britain*, ed. D. B. Harden, London, 1956, pp. ix–xxi: this volume of papers in his honour also contains a complete bibliography of his writings. The significance of *The Archaeology of the Anglo-Saxon Settlements* is well discussed in this sympathetic memoir and I am much indebted to its authors, Dr. D. B. Harden and Mr. R. L. S. Bruce-Mitford, both of whom knew Leeds well, as indeed, to my great advantage, I did myself.

did not come out until 1915, and R. A. Smith's *Guide to the Anglo-Saxon Antiquities in the British Museum* is dated 1923. It is true that Smith's masterly chapters in the Victoria County History had covered the Anglo-Saxon remains of twenty-one counties by 1912, but they only summarized the contents of central and local museums and the work of earlier scholars, without providing any general synthesis. It is significant of the unfamiliarity of the subject to historians in 1913 that Leeds felt it necessary at an early point in his book (pp. 24–5) to demonstrate that the antiquities he proposed to discuss were really Anglo-Saxon, and to challenge (p. 12) Oman's then recently published claim that 'the spade, so useful in the Roman period, helps us little here.'[1]

It is difficult to appreciate nowadays the novelty of much that Leeds packed into this little book in 1913. Not only did he include a lucid account of the main principles of archaeological method—the establishment of typological series, their relative dating by groups of associated objects, the importance of distributions in determining patterns of settlement—but he showed for the first time how all these factors could contribute significantly to our historical knowledge of the early Anglo-Saxon centuries. The arrangement of the book, with five of its seven chapters devoted to separate consideration of the Angles, the Saxons, and the Jutes, and their respective continental origins, involved a comparative study of the English and European material on a scale never before attempted in such detail.[2] This led him not merely to distinguish some features of the Saxon *Kulturkreis* between the Elbe and the Weser from those of more northerly continental antecedents, such as the cruciform brooches, which he rightly associated with the Angles, but to call attention to the links between the culture of Kent

---

[1] *England before the Norman Conquest* (1910), 187.

[2] In this as in other ways Leeds was treading in the footsteps of J. M. Kemble who had attempted before 1850 to demonstrate the continental homes of the English by conducting excavations in north German cemeteries and comparing the material in continental museums with that found in this country. See his pioneer paper in *Archaeologia*, xxxvi (1856), reprinted in *Horae Ferales* (1863).

and that of the Frankish Rhineland, and so raise all the complex issues that surround the problem of the Jutes. Leeds had a very wide knowledge of the continental literature then available to illustrate these questions and, while much of what he wrote now looks superficial and even misleading in the light of more recent research, he was the first to show the relevance to our Anglo-Saxon antiquities of such fundamental concepts as the distinction drawn by Salin between the different styles of animal ornament,[1] or the typological analysis of cruciform brooches devised by Schetelig in Norway.[2]

In applying this knowledge to the English scene Leeds reached several conclusions which have played a major part in the subsequent development of the subject. Of the greatest general importance perhaps was his claim (p. 95) that 'a large number of the settlements must have come into being considerably earlier than any historical documents will warrant'. In this he was entirely right, and his publication here (pp. 55-7 and fig. 8) of the Dorchester burials, though their true meaning eluded him, and everyone else, until 1954,[3] well illustrates his instinct for seeing the special significance of objects unimpressive in themselves. His use of this and other evidence to demonstrate the very early date of Saxon settlement in the Upper Thames valley forced on the reluctant attention of historians the necessity for a reappraisal of current notions on the origins of Wessex. It has already been noted how his demonstration of the strongly Frankish

[1] B. Salin, *Die Altgermanische Thierornamentik* (1904). It will be noted that Leeds here (p. 35) follows Salin in dating the beginnings of Style I about 450. More recent work, notably that of E. Bakka, *On the Beginning of . . . Style I in England* (1958), suggests that this is too early. If Style I began around 500, some difficulties felt by Leeds disappear, notably that of placing the earliest types of saucer brooch before its inception: see his discussion of Sussex, pp. 45-8.

[2] H. Schetelig, *The Cruciform Brooches of Norway* (1908). It has to be remembered that in discussing the chronology of these brooches in England (p. 76) Leeds was writing long before the publication of N. Åberg, *The Anglo-Saxons in England* (1926), whose typology and dating has been followed by most recent scholars.

[3] See his article, with Joan Kirk, in *Oxoniensia*, xvii/xviii (1954), 63-76.

influence on the archaeology of Kent compelled a similar reappraisal of the Jutish problem, though this was destined to arouse far greater difficulties of interpretation than Leeds, or anyone else, could have foreseen in 1913. Of equal importance in stimulating discussion was his use of distribution maps to show, for example, how in most parts of eastern England the pattern of settlement seemed to be determined rather by the use of rivers than of Roman roads (pp. 16–17) or to indicate the extent of Saxon influence over wide areas in the eastern midlands that tradition and nomenclature alike had hitherto assigned to the Angles (pp. 78–81).

His account of these and many other aspects of the Anglo-Saxon settlement to which he was the first to direct attention has of course inevitably been outmoded to a greater or lesser extent by the passage of time. It is no longer true, as it was in 1913, that 'not a single instance of an early Anglo-Saxon occupation-area . . . has ever been brought to light in this country' (p. 15): Leeds's own pioneer excavation of the village site at Sutton Courtenay, Berks., was soon to make that statement obsolete,[1] and his example has been followed on a widening scale elsewhere, so that the archaeology of the age is no longer so completely dependent on the evidence of grave-goods as it then was. More evidence for cremation in Essex and Sussex can now be adduced than Leeds was ready to admit: nor can it any longer be stated that 'in the whole of Hampshire, outside the Jutish district, not a single [Saxon] cemetery is known' (p. 51).[2] His view that 'the difficulties in the way of equating the archaeological remains of any Saxon district in England with those of any particular part of North Germany are very great' (p. 96) is no longer valid, since, quite apart from the ceramic evidence, which Leeds ignored, the continental distribution of such types

[1] *Archaeologia*, lxxiii (1923), 147–92 ; lxxvi (1927), 59–80 ; xcii (1947), 79–93.

[2] Apart from the substantial cemeteries, not yet published, at Worthy Park and Winnall, near Winchester, cremation urns are known from Fareham, occupation debris from Portchester Castle, and small groups of inhumations from several other sites: see A. Meaney, *A Gazetteer of Early Anglo-Saxon Burial Sites* (1964), 94–103.

INTRODUCTION TO 1970 REPRINT

as saucer brooches and equal-armed brooches, which he
recognized as Saxon, has become much clearer since 1913.
The whole question of the Jutes has been copiously discussed
from many angles since it was first raised by Leeds in the
last two chapters of this book, and his own views on it were
radically altered more than once in later years:[1] what he
wrote here in Chapters VI and VII raised some problems
which are not yet wholly solved. But these chapters retain
a period interest as the first demonstration of a number of
puzzles presented by the Dark-Age antiquities of Kent; they
had the great merit of provoking fruitful discussion which is,
however slowly, leading to a deeper understanding of several
aspects not only of English but of European archaeology in
this age.

Leeds's book had, however, certain basic defects which
should not be overlooked. Even on the archaeological side
he did not use all the evidence that was available in 1913.
Throughout his life Leeds had a blind spot for pottery,
remarkable in one who spent so much of his time with
Museum collections and was well aware how much information on the earlier pre-historic periods had been obtained
from ceramic studies. His flair for extracting a meaningful
arrangement from a group of broken bronze fragments or a
significant typology from a series of brooches or buckles,
was unrivalled, but his interest was liable to flag if he was
confronted with a box of potsherds or even a row of cremation
urns. A phrase on p. 118 where he refers casually to 'a
few cremation urns and other unimportant objects', gives a
quite unconscious but revealing insight into his lack of
interest in what pottery might tell him. Although he included

[1] This development can be traced in the two chapters devoted to the
'Kentish Problem' in his *Early Anglo-Saxon Art and Archaeology*
(1936), in his article on 'Denmark and Early England' in *Ant. Journ.*,
xxvi (1946), 31–7, and the note on 'Anglo-Saxon Exports' in *Ant.
Journ.*, xxxiii (1953), 208–10. For the latest stage of his thought, see
the posthumously published 'Notes on Jutish Art in Kent': edited by
Sonia Chadwick, in *Mediaeval Archaeology*, i (1957), 5–26. It will be
seen that by 1955 Leeds had come to recognize significant Jutish, or at
least Scandinavian, influences in Kent, whose existence he had altogether
denied in 1913.

an excellent photograph of the urn from Tradescant's Ark, now in the Ashmolean (fig. 5), which may have been one of the 'sad sepulchral pitchers' that provoked Sir Thomas Browne into the writing of his *Hydriotaphia*, he did so purely for its historical associations and with no reference whatever to its typology. Some sixty years earlier J. M. Kemble had pointed out the similarities between some English cremation urns and those from the neighbourhood of Stade in the Elbe valley, and many of the latter, with subsequent discoveries, are still at Hanover and in the other German museums that Leeds knew well, but he made no attempt to follow up these clues. Had he done so, he would have found reinforcement for many of the conclusions to which his work on the metal objects was pointing, especially perhaps for the presence of fifth-century Saxon elements among the settlers of East and Middle Anglia. He could, moreover, very easily have produced a distribution map of continental urn-types vastly superior in meaning to fig. 16 which shows nothing but a crude and perfunctory distinction between Saxon and Frankish pottery, with nothing at all from Angle Schleswig or from Jutland.[1]

By thus ignoring the evidence of pottery Leeds inevitably gave a distorted picture of the settlement of eastern England. He pays no attention to the phenomenon presented by the areas, principally in Norfolk, Lincolnshire, and east Yorkshire, that are dominated by great cremation cemeteries, containing few or no inhumation burials. In view of his references to the continental urn-fields in Schleswig and Hanover (pp. 88–90), this is a very odd omission, all the more so because, throughout his period at the Ashmolean, his department there housed a very long run of urns from one of the greatest of the English cremation cemeteries, that at

[1] It is, however, only fair to remember that the first major study of the German pottery on modern typological and chronological lines, A. Plettke's, *Ursprung und Ausbreitung der Angeln und Sachsen*, was not published until 1920. Leeds, however, was well acquainted with the earlier literature, including J. Mestorf, *Urnenfriedhöfe in Schleswig-Holstein* (1886) which he used (pp. 87–9), in describing the Borgstedt cemetery.

Sancton in east Yorkshire, which in fact is nowhere mentioned in this book. In most of his references to cremation in the English cemeteries Leeds is concerned to stress either what he elsewhere termed 'the flight from cremation' during the pagan period, or the occasional instances of its persistence as late as the seventh century (p. 74). At no point does he discuss its significance in those areas where it dominated the cemeteries or inquire what light the cremation urns themselves might throw on the date at which the settlements began or the regions on the continent from which the earliest settlers were derived.

A much more serious blemish, and one which was properly criticized by historians, was the very cavalier treatment which Leeds gave to the literary sources for the period. He was of course primarily concerned to make a case for the serious consideration of archaeological evidence by historians who were inclined to follow Oman in ignoring or belittling the contribution it could make to an understanding of this age. In doing this he was on firm ground, and so long as he stuck to the archaeological material which he knew so well it was difficult to deny the force of his arguments. But he greatly weakened his own credibility in the eyes of historians by carelessness and inaccuracy in his references to the literary sources. Thus (p. 50) he writes of a West Saxon landing recorded 'in 504 at Porta, which name is suggestive of the modern Portsmouth'. This is a garbled version of the Anglo-Saxon Chronicle entry not for 504 but for 501, which mentions the arrival of one Port and his sons at Portesmutha. Similarly (p. 50) he turns the British king Natanleod mentioned in the Annal for 508 into 'a battle at Natanleod, identified with Netley', and in the same context interpolates 'the series of battles linked with the name of Arthur culminating . . . at Mons Badonicus' between the Chronicle entries for 519 and 552, without explaining that they are derived not from the Chronicle at all but from the *Historia Brittonum*, and without apparently realizing that a date for Mons Badonicus as late as the middle of the sixth century is quite unacceptable on other grounds. He writes of the Isle of Wight (p. 116) that in 530 'it was overrun by the West Saxons . . . with great slaughter of its existing occupiers at Withgarasbyrig and handed over by Cerdic to Withgar. It is not heard of again until A.D. 681'. In fact there is no record of a great slaughter in 530, when the Chronicle merely notes that Cerdic and Cynric 'slew a few men at Wihtgarasbyrg': the handing over to Stuf and Wihtgar is noted later under 534, and the death of Wihtgar ten years later still. On p. 118 this mythical 'slaughter of the inhabitants' in 530, which may derive from a confusion in Leeds's mind with the activities of Cædwalla of Wessex a century and a half later, as recorded by Bede, is mentioned again as providing a possible contradiction with the continuously Jutish (Kentish) character of the Island's culture both before and after that date.[1] Apart from these misquotations Leeds could be curiously inaccurate over matters of historic fact: when, for example, he wrote (p. 22) that 'all the bishoprics connected with Roman towns were established before A.D. 700', he must have temporarily forgotten at least the medieval sees of Chichester, Exeter, and Carlisle. It was not perhaps surprising that some historians, confronted with such lapses on matters with which they were familiar, continued to treat with a degree of scepticism Leeds's claims that archaeology could provide a more accurate account of early Anglo-Saxon history than the literary sources whose evidence he so needlessly abused.

It is right to draw attention, on the occasion of its reprinting, to the defects in a book whose merits as a whole are so singular and whose influence both on historical and archaeological studies has been so great. Anyone reading it for the first time, or rereading it after a lapse of years, should be on guard against accepting its detail uncritically or paying too

---

[1] There is a double confusion here, for, according to Asser's Life of King Alfred, Stuf and Wihtgar, from whom Alfred's mother claimed descent, were themselves Jutes. So far, therefore, from the events of 530 having extirpated a Jutish population in the Island, as Leeds wrongly suggested, they are more likely to have been the origin of the Jutish (Kentish) elements there which he was concerned to emphasize. No reliance can of course be placed on the exact dates attributed by the Chronicle to the traditions which it records in this period.

INTRODUCTION TO 1970 REPRINT

great regard to errors of fact or eccentricities of interpretation. In a subject that has grown over the past half-century, with a vigour that Leeds himself did so much to stimulate, it is surprising indeed that a book written in 1913 should still be thought worth reprinting in its original form. That it should be so reprinted is a tribute to its lasting value, a tribute moreover to the enduring influence of a notable character and a scholar of great perspicacity.

J. N. L. MYRES

Christ Church, Oxford.

PREFACE

THE aim of this little work is to put forward the problems of early Anglo-Saxon archeology in a connected form, in the hope that it may prove of service to those engaged in the study of the period. If anything, beyond the attraction of the antiquities for their own sake, has prompted the author to undertake the task, it is the ordinary attitude of writers in other fields of Anglo-Saxon research towards the archaeological remains. Professor Chadwick is probably the only writer who has incorporated in a general work on the origin of the Anglo-Saxons any measure of archaeological evidence, but welcome as his brief notice is, it touches but a few points. The more usual course has been to pass over archaeological research in a single paragraph or to make a few disjointed references to its conclusions or to ignore them altogether. Possibly archaeology is to a large extent to blame in that it has attempted in recent years no general survey of the material in keeping with the advanced ideas demanded by modern scientific methods. The whole subject has been dismissed in one column in Hoops' *Reallexikon der Germanischen Altertumskunde* under the heading *Angelsächsische Funde*, where the information is largely based on De Baye's *Industrie Anglo-Saxonne*, a somewhat antiquated work and not always correct. A further article on *Englisches Siedelungswesen* hardly treats the matter seriously. In the following pages some attempt has been made to fill this blank, especially in regard to the correlation of English and Continental material, which has necessarily a most important bearing on the question of the origins of the Anglo-Saxon race. So

far as possible, the problems have been discussed on broad
lines, and occasional lapses from this principle must be
attributed to the somewhat restricted character of the
material. It would not be fair to leave unacknowledged the
extent to which the compilation of such a work as this is
facilitated nowadays by the articles on Anglo-Saxon remains
in the *Victoria County Histories*, on which the map (fig. 1)
is largely based. These articles, mainly the work of Mr.
Reginald A. Smith of the British Museum, suffer, however, in
one respect from the arbitrary limitations imposed upon them
by restricting discussion to the antiquities discovered within
the individual counties, as the county divisions, being a product of a later time, have nothing in common with the diffusion
of the tribes which constituted the early English. The real
value of these articles consists in the collection of the scattered
bibliography of Anglo-Saxon archaeology. But as some of the
most important counties still remain to be edited, this bibliography is not yet complete. Further, there is no English
work dealing with the Continental material, and a large part of
the German finds of the period having never been published
in a detailed manner are only accessible to study at first-hand.
The subjects for many of the illustrations have been taken
from objects now in the Ashmolean Museum, but the author
has to acknowledge his indebtedness to the Council of the
Society of Antiquaries for the loan of the blocks of figures
3, 4, 8, 9 and 15, to the Council of the Kent Archaeological
Society for permission to reproduce figure 21, and for several
photographs of objects in the Society's collection. Thanks
are also due to the Council of the *Victoria County Histories*
for permission to reproduce figure 7, and to Dr. Salin,
Riksantikvariet at Stockholm, for similar permission in regard
to figures 2, 3 and 23. The photographs for figures 17 and 18
have kindly been supplied by the Directions of the Museums
at Hanover and Leeuwarden. Finally, the author desires to

express his deep gratitude to all those who have assisted in the recent excavations at Alfriston, Sussex, for allowing him to anticipate in some measure the publication of the extremely important finds which those excavations have produced. That permission has enabled the author to put forward some new ideas which were only suggested by seeing the Alfriston finds. Not all the conclusions in this work are new, but in every case they are advanced afresh after personal examination of the material on which they are based.

Thanks are due to Mr. D. G. Hogarth, who has kindly read the proofs and offered several valuable criticisms and suggestions.

E. THURLOW LEEDS.

Oxford, *June* 1913.

CONTENTS

LIST OF ILLUSTRATIONS

CHAPTER I

INTRODUCTORY AND GEOGRAPHICAL CONSIDERATIONS

THE period of the coming of the Anglo-Saxons is certainly
one of the most tantalizing in the whole history of the British
Isles—or perhaps more correctly speaking of England, as the
events, of which the archaeological material remains as
tangible evidence, had practically speaking no immediate
reference to other parts of these islands. By the time that
the Romans finally evacuated Britain, it might be said that
the dark ages of prehistory had yielded to an era in which
both history and archaeology contribute their quota to the
store of knowledge concerning the manners and customs of
the daily life of the inhabitants of this country. But this
brighter age was destined to receive a check in its development. The departure of the Romans and the coming of the
Teutonic invaders mark a reversion to an obscurity such as
enfolds the last centuries before the Christian era, but, while
in this latter case it is necessary, apart from the one brief
account of the journey of Pytheas of Massilia, to reconstruct
the history of the period from a study of the archaeological
remains in the light of the corresponding material of the
Continent and the records of contemporary events handed
down by classical writers, for the Teutonic invasion of Britain
there is no lack of historical records. These records, however,
are for the most part of the barest nature, consisting of loose
statements of facts, many bearing the unmistakable stamp of
strong partiality, or of obscure passages in Continental writers
who had no immediate interest in the concerns of Britain, and
who consequently did not trouble much to aspire to absolute
accuracy. The records which do exist are more often than

not mutually contradictory, and it is perhaps only necessary to contemplate the enormous amount of learning which has been devoted to the study of the history, language, and social institutions of the earliest English to realize what a fascination and yet what difficulties surround the elucidation of the problems of this important period. Of the historians, only Gildas (*c*. 540 A.D.), Procopius (*c*. 550), Zosimus (sixth century), and the writer usually known as Prosper Tiro(*c*. 450)can in any way be regarded as contemporary, and even then with one exception they all wrote nearly a century after the first arrival of the English. The three last named contributed nothing beyond about one isolated statement apiece. Gildas's account, though interesting, has all the appearance of a work based on traditions which had already been passed on by several mouths and those by no means impartial. For the rest, namely Bede, the author of the *Historia Brittonum* and the *Anglo-Saxon Chronicle*, they are all of later date and nothing is known of the actual sources of their information, though the last is conjectured to have drawn largely upon Bede. The fullest accounts are given by Bede and the *Chronicle*, but the events recorded for the first two-hundred years of English history are almost entirely confined to the dates of important battles, and those of the accession and death of the ruling chiefs, and these simple facts only admit of somewhat general conclusions. Again, even the dates of these events do not agree in every account, but, such as they are, they can, together with the names of the places at which the battles were fought, be found in any text-book of English history, and it would be entirely a work of supererogation to repeat them here. After the lapse of a certain length of time—that is to say, when the events recorded are contemporary or only just antecedent to the date of the actual chronicler—they are given in greater detail, and although some obscurity is still in evidence, yet it is as nothing in comparison with that which envelops the infancy of the Anglo-Saxon race.

At this point it is essential to state clearly the exact period of time which the present work is intended to cover, and this involves a further statement of one outstanding event, namely, the conversion of the new race from heathenism to Christianity. The chroniclers have a good deal to record in one way or another in connexion with this important change in religious beliefs, but in the main they confine themselves to a record of missionary activities, often of the rivalries between existing schools of thought, and of the dates of the baptism of royal houses. Of the effect of the missionaries' teaching on the population as a whole only a general idea can be formed. But it seems to be generally admitted that the acceptance of Christianity involved a further important change, though the exact moment at which the change took place, or rather the length of time which was necessary for its complete accomplishment, is a matter of considerable doubt. The innovation in question is the removal of the burying-ground from the open country to the enceinte of the churchyard. There is no reason to suppose that the pagan grave-field was enshrouded by any less degree of sanctity than the 'God's-acre', but it is evident that the Christian priesthood considered it absolutely essential to institute the change as a method of weaning their flocks as far as possible from every association with their former beliefs and superstitions. It is generally supposed that the institution of churchyard-burial belongs to the early part of the eighth century, and, as will appear subsequently, the latest actual evidences of pagan burial do not extend beyond the middle of the seventh century. That is the latest period for which archaeology bears witness to such burial; the interval between the cessation of interment in the open country and the permanent institution of the churchyard is a blank for which positive evidence is entirely wanting. It has been suggested that the practice of burying in the open country still persisted, but unaccompanied by the deposition of relics in the graves, and that in this manner the transition period can be covered. Possibly some of the very poorly furnished graves with easterly orientation in Anglo-Saxon cemeteries may represent this transition period, but it is a pure conjecture, and a constant series of naked graves in these pagan cemeteries has still to be proved. It is thus the period extending from the first coming of the invaders down to the cessation of the evidence furnished by the pagan burials that it is purposed to deal with in the following pages. The why and wherefore of the limitation of the inquiry to this brief period will be discussed shortly. For the moment, it is only necessary to utter a protest against the historian's attitude towards Anglo-Saxon archaeology. A good example of that attitude is to be found in Professor Oman's *England before the Norman Conquest*. He says (p. 187):

'The spade, so useful in the Roman period, helps us little here; the Teutonic invader has left us no inscriptions earlier than the year 600; his British enemies hardly any and those of the shortest. Saxon graves of the pagan period give us a good deal of information concerning the social life and culture of the incoming race, but not definite history: in that respect they can only be used like the barrows of the Britons who lived before Julius Caesar.'

There is, perhaps, a good deal of truth in this opinion, but on the other hand it conveys a very false idea of the value of Anglo-Saxon archaeology. Roman archaeology in England may be said to cover a period of 400 years, and even apart from the history or inscriptions much could be learnt from it by mere comparison with Continental material. The Anglo-Saxon remains cover little more than 200 years, and though by no means so varied in character, nor supported by very reliable records, yet they furnish valuable evidence of the movements of the invaders, because close comparison is possible with similar remains on the Continent, many of which can be dated with certainty and for which also there exists a reliable historical background. The greatest misconception lies in the attempt to draw a parallel between Anglo-Saxon relics and those of the pre-Roman period. The former are, even at the present time, very numerous and are confined to two centuries, belonging to the age of definite history and connected with a limited area, while in the latter case, to go no farther back even than the end of the Stone Age, the remains are no more numerous and have to be spread over at least two thousand years, during most of which the course of events in Western Europe, from an historical aspect, lies in absolute darkness.

What then is the material available for archaeological study during early Anglo-Saxon times? Such as it is, it stands out in strong contrast to that available from the preceding Roman period, and the root of the difference lies in the origins, customs, and the very natures of the peoples represented by the two cultures. The Roman occupation of Britain was part and parcel of the extension of a great Empire, and was essentially military in character. It was marked by the construction of military high-roads, forming a network across the country. The terminal points of those roads, and the principal points of intersection, were marked by strongly fortified towns, portions at least of whose walls in many cases stand to the present time to bear witness to the skilful masons and engineers whose services the Roman conquerors could command. The remains of villas, scattered here and there in the south, testify to the more peaceful aspect of the occupation. In short, they are all part of one huge system. Equally so are the smaller remains which are turned up in almost every square yard of English soil. Their keynote is homogeneity; here and there slight local differences can be noted, but in the main the Roman culture is one and the same throughout all the Western Provinces of the Empire. But there is another side to the picture of the Roman occupation of Britain, and that is its transitory nature. What permanent effect did it have on the country? The answer must be 'practically none'. From the Latin tongue a few words survived in the English Language; and from the Roman legal system some traces remained, notably in the customary law of London; the design of the earliest Anglo-Saxon money was derived from Roman coin-types; and here and there faint traces of Roman art can be detected in the first products of Anglo-Saxon culture. But the Romans came and went, and with them vanished practically everything that they had toiled so hard to impress upon the country—institutions, language, and culture; all their labour in vain; only their massive masonry, a fitting emblem of the domination of Rome, still thrust itself upwards to bear silent witness that once the Roman Legions had conquered Britain.

What then of the Anglo-Saxons ? They were all that the Romans were not, and yet they left behind them a lasting heritage. They came in the first instance not as a proud military power seeking fresh fields to conquer, but in search of loot and plunder, mere bands of ravening pirates. So long as the Romans could hold them in check, they got no further, but once the Legions were withdrawn, they descended in hordes on the shores of Britain—like the Romans, to conquer; but, unlike the Romans, to stay. Force of circumstances, or natural bent, drove them to seek a new home ; they came as true immigrants ; they occupied the country, and by a gradual process of absorption they made England their own. And their success lay in their manner of life. They were not a military race, though warlike ; once they had conquered they settled down to the life of village communities, introducing their own particular systems of land-tenure, not as exploiters but as owners of the soil, with a definite personal attachment to it. But they came as isolated bands or septs under their special leader, serving their own ends ; they sprang from the whole length of the southern coasts of the North Sea ; and thus the keynote of the Anglo-Saxon settlements is heterogeneity. At first intercommunication was scarce, as intertribal hostility was rife, and though the new-comers used the Roman roads they hardly troubled to keep them in repair; but they *made* no roads, though often they struck out fresh trackways for themselves. It is doubtful whether much trade existed ; indeed the law of Withraed of Kent, which bade a stranger approaching a village otherwise than by a road to blow a horn or shout, proves clearly that even for some time after the settlements had become an established fact, all 'foreigners' were apt to be viewed with mistrust. It is in their material culture, however, that the strongest contrast exists. They left no monuments in stone like the Romans, simply because they did not understand the working of stone; they came, for the most part, of a race which has always excelled in wood-work. All their houses, certainly those of any size, were constructed entirely of wood, like the hall at Heorot, so vividly described in *Beowulf*, perhaps in some cases with a foundation and lower course of rough masonry, as in the church at Greenstead, Essex, almost the only surviving example of true Anglo-Saxon architecture.

There is further an entire absence of written records—whether on parchment, wood, or stone—at least until the close of the seventh century. The system of writing in use was the runes, unsuited for anything but the briefest inscriptions. Doubtless many such inscriptions did exist, principally on wood, for which the system was particularly adapted, but these have all perished; only a few sparse examples on metal—such as a brooch from Gilton, Kent—have survived. Their own method of recording events was certainly by oral tradition, and though much of that tradition may have been collected into their writings by the monkish chroniclers, there can be no guarantee of its absolute accuracy.

Where their settlements were, can be surmised in a large measure from the place-names, but in the majority of cases it is impossible to fix even approximately between the first arrival and the Domesday Book the date at which those settlements were established. That they stood on the site of the village or town which stills bears their name is more than probable, but again there is no definite proof of it, as all traces of any original buildings have perished, and in some cases at least the village has probably grown up round the Christian church, which may have been built at some distance from the site of the pagan settlement. This even is conjectural, as apart from the absence of original buildings, not a single instance of an early Anglo-Saxon occupation-area vouched for by the discovery of sherds or the like, such as litter the ground of any Roman site, has ever been brought to light in this country. Apart from a few earthworks which have been attributed to Anglo-Saxon activities, and those for the most

part doubtful, nothing remains above ground to bear witness
that, when the Anglo-Saxons occupied any given district, they
selected one particular spot in preference to another.

It may be asked then, What have the Anglo-Saxon invaders
left behind them to serve as a basis for archaeological study?
The answer is, their cemeteries, nothing more and nothing less.
They are the sole tangible evidence of their existence, and to
that extent such a stricture on Anglo-Saxon archaeology as that
quoted above may appear at first sight to be amply justified.
One reason for contesting that idea has already been put
forward and there are others which may now be considered.
Much can be learnt which is of value in reconstructing the
history of this obscure period—firstly, from the distribution of
these cemeteries, and secondly, from their contents.

Firstly, then, as to their distribution. Such cemeteries as
are known—for doubtless many still remain to be brought to
light—definitely mark the presence of an early settlement in
the immediate neighbourhood, and it is not a little instructive
to note how their position was chosen with all due consideration to the physical and other advantages which were offered
by the particular site. It will be found that while there is
a large element of truth in the description which Tacitus gives
of the method of settlement among the Germanic tribes, in
some respects it is clear that the historian did not entirely
realize the facts of the case. He says ' colunt discreti ac diversi,
ut fons, ut campus, ut nemus placuit '.[1] The first part of the
description pictures clearly the scattered communities which
were involved by the system of land-tenure, but the second part
would suggest a very haphazard manner of choosing the site of
a settlement, and that, at least so far as the Anglo-Saxons were
concerned, is assuredly incorrect, as careful examination will
show that in practically every case full account was taken of
some natural advantage, such as proximity to a ford, an easily
defended position, and, most important of all, a dry subsoil.
It has been stated above that, at any rate, at first there was
little or no intercommunication between the immigrating

[1] *Germania* xvi.

tribes, and this suggests first a consideration of the position of the settlements in regard to the lines of natural or artificial communication. To take the latter first, it has been observed that the Anglo-Saxon villages, almost without exception, lie at some little distance from the line of any adjacent Roman road. Professor Baldwin Brown [1] aptly instances the Roman road from Bourne to the Humber, along the whole length of which not a single village bearing a Saxon name can be found on the actual road itself. All lie at least half a mile distant to the right or left. It is a curious but undoubted fact, that the Teutonic settlers seem to have carefully avoided planting their settlements on such roads. The reason is not always quite clear, but in the main it lies in the fact that the Roman road-system, being entirely military in character, drove straight across country, for the most part avoiding the lower lands abutting on a river or stream which offered the greatest advantages for settlements of an agricultural nature such as were those of the Anglo-Saxons. And this avoidance may possibly have been further prompted by the greater liability to attack by roving bands of hostile tribes, to whom the Roman roads would offer a swift and easy progress. And herein lies perhaps the most important point which has to be borne in mind in dealing with the question of the Anglo-Saxon immigrations. The sharpest distinction must be drawn between incursions of armed piratical bands, moving rapidly across country, leaving ruin and havoc in their train, such as are pictured so vividly in what have been aptly described as the ' hysterical periods of Gildas ', and bands of immigrants proper, bringing with them their wives and children, their Lares and Penates and all their worldly possessions. To the former the Roman roads would afford unparalleled advantages for rapid movement ; along their course the Roman towns and villas, which would be the goal of the German pirates, could easily be reached, and at the same time they would secure for them an easy retreat in the event of repulse at any given point in their advance. It is certain, however,

---

[1] *The Arts in Early England,* i. 60.

that in the latter case these roads would be little used; the immigrants were essentially a seafaring race; from them sprang the pirates against whom the 'Saxons shores', both in France and England, had been instituted; they swarmed across to Britain in their 'long keels' or other shallow-draft vessels similar to that discovered in the moor at Nydam in Schleswig, and akin to those in which the Norsemen in 916 penetrated up the Ouse to Tempsford and beyond. Such were the means by which the immigrants pushed their way into the heart of Britain, and thus it is that nearly all the principal settlements of this early period are to be found in close proximity to some navigable stream or along the course of some tributary leading directly from it. In the consideration of the earliest occupation of this country by the Anglo-Saxons, hardly too great stress can be laid on the importance of the river-systems as the key by means of which the whole distribution of the settlements can be solved. A map showing the positions of the burial-places of this period bears this out in the most striking manner (fig. 1); occasional anomalies may be observable, but they are merely the exceptions which prove the rule. Equally, such a map, if superimposed on one showing the Roman roads, will demonstrate that, in spite of the network spread by the latter over the whole country, only here and there are any settlements to be found of which it might be said that the roads were the way by which their occupiers came. More often than not, such roads follow closely the line of the alternative river-route. A good example is furnished by the two roads in the vicinity of East Stoke and Burton, running almost parallel to the Trent, but the prior claim of the river seems here to be proved by the presence of a thick cluster of cemeteries close to the river between the two points mentioned, at which the two roads severally strike away from the course of the river.

The avoidance of things Roman does not appear, however, to have been confined to the road-system; it is also noteworthy that Anglo-Saxon cemeteries are but seldom found in proximity to a Roman town, certainly none of any size. One

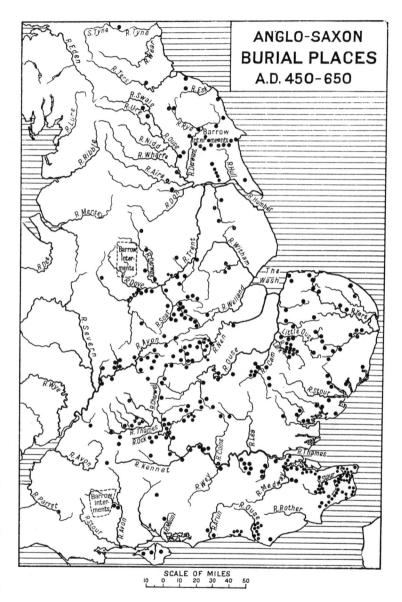

ANGLO-SAXON
BURIAL PLACES
A.D. 450-650

SCALE OF MILES
10   0   10   20   30   40   50

Fig. 1.

of the most difficult problems in connexion with the Anglo-
Saxon occupation of Britain is the question of the destruction
of many of the Roman towns.   It is little short of remarkable
that in the earliest records of events, no towns are mentioned,
except places for the most part of secondary importance, in
the west of England.   London is only casually mentioned,
Canterbury (Durovernum) merely in connexion with Augus-
tine, while such important towns as Colchester (Camalo-
dunum), St. Albans (Verulamium), Winchester (Venta Bel-
garum), and York (Eboracum) are almost as if they had never
existed at all. That, after the departure of the Legions, many
of them were ransacked and put to fire and the sword is
certain, but who were the perpetrators in each individual
case is far from clear.   It is more than probable that, owing
to the description of the invaders given by writers like Gildas,
the Teutonic tribes have been credited with the destruction
of some towns without sufficient justification, whilst the
absolute oblivion in which the ultimate fate of places like
Silchester and Verulamium is enveloped would suggest that
they fell before the early piratical raids, and not to the
settlers who followed them.[1]   No Anglo-Saxon cemeteries
have been found anywhere near them ; that closest to Silchester, which lay on the Roman road from London to
Sarum, is at Reading, a good instance of the Saxons' preference for a river site.   The largest number of cemeteries just
outside the limits of Roman settlements is to be found in
Kent, but this, as will appear from the account of the Kentish
finds, may be attributed partly to the density of the population and partly to causes to be sought for in the origin of the
Kentish settlers themselves, a point which may be reserved
until the final chapter, where this subject will be dealt with
more fully.   Elsewhere, the establishment of the communal
village at some little distance from the site of the Roman
town is particularly noticeable, and it is possible that the
reason lies in some such superstition or custom as preserved
the moor-finds of North Germany and Scandinavia intact

[1] *Cambridge Mediaeval History*, i. 380.

until they were laid bare by the archaeologist's spade in recent times. Thus it would seem to have been with deliberate intent, possibly merely strategical, that the Saxons established themselves on the farther bank of the Wiltshire Avon at Harnham Hill, just west of the modern Salisbury, and some two miles from Old Sarum, the site of the Roman Sorbiodunum.[1] But there may also have existed a desire to place water between themselves and the ghosts which might be thought to haunt a spot which they had put to fire and the sword. Against this, however, has to be ranged the undoubted fact that not a few cemeteries are situated but a short distance from Roman villas, as at Wheatley, Oxfordshire, and Frilford, Berkshire, or again, the frequency with which graves of Anglo-Saxons are found in close contiguity to those of their Roman predecessors. In the matter of the Roman towns there is no reason to suppose that in some of them at least, some measure of communal life has not survived unbroken from Roman times. The evidence for this seems particularly strong in the case of London, where the customary law, notably that of inheritance which came into being during the Roman domination, still remained in force within the bounds of the City right down to the eighteenth century.[2] But, so far as the Anglo-Saxons are concerned, it is not until the coming of the missionaries that the former Roman towns begin to figure once more in the history of the country. The reason for this resurrection, as it were, is not far to seek. The missionaries commissioned by the Roman Church with the conversion of the heathen Teutonic tribes, would naturally arrive imbued with all the traditions of the Roman occupation, and would thus seek to establish themselves at centres in which the Roman atmosphere could most easily be revived. It was the missionaries, too, who re-introduced into England the practice of building in stone, in the first instance

---

[1] According to the latest reports, there is little evidence that the Romans occupied Old Sarum itself. Their head-quarters appear to have been at Stratford, close by.

[2] Sir L. Gomme, *The Making of London*, p. 91.

merely for the erection of sacred buildings, and thus in time
arose once more on the sites of the former Roman towns,
cities and towns which have enjoyed a continuous existence
down to the present day.   Not all of the early bishoprics,
however, were established on ancient Roman sites [1] ; of those
existing before A. D. 700 no less than nine out of sixteen were
connected with places which only had come into existence
under the Anglo-Saxons, but the strength of the Roman
tradition is in no way better exemplified than by the removal
to Winchester in 662 of the bishopric of Wessex, at first
identified with the place of the baptism of Cynegils, the
West-Saxon king, namely Dorchester in Oxfordshire, itself
nevertheless a small post in Roman times.   All the bishoprics
connected with Roman towns were established before
A. D. 700.

There are other minor points bearing on the distribution of
the Anglo-Saxon settlements as evidenced by the cemeteries
which deserve brief mention.   The choice of a suitable subsoil has already been noticed, and in this connexion it is
remarkable how closely the geological conditions bear out
the wisdom which prompted the selection of any given site.
Particular attention has been drawn to the positions of the
settlements in Northamptonshire at the junction of the
Lower Lias clay and the Northampton Sands, where not only
a dry subsoil could be assured, but also abundance of water.[2]
The application of this criterion to Anglo-Saxon occupation-
areas is peculiarly instructive as demonstrating the close
communion with nature in which the invaders, like most
semi-civilized and primitive peoples, lived.   The close adherence
to the lines of the river-system noted above serves further to
explain the fact that, in the majority of cases, the early boundaries between the different tribes are coterminous with the
line of important watersheds.   Here and there this statement
would seem to conflict with the records of the early historians, but when the archaeological evidence comes to be tested,

[1] G. Baldwin Brown, *The Arts in Early England*, i. 20.
[2] *V. C. H.*, *Northants*, i. 226.

it will be seen that most, if not all, of these apparent contradictions disappear.

The importance of some of the considerations advanced above in connexion with the study of the archaeology of this period may seem at first sight to have been somewhat over-estimated, and, if it had been a question of the immigration of a tribe or tribes, who had lived for some time previously amidst the civilizing influences of the Roman Empire, the accusation would have contained a large measure of truth. The Teutonic invaders, however, have been often bluntly termed barbarians, and even if this appellation be somewhat strong, yet their culture, institutions, and beliefs all betoken a race occupying a comparatively low place in the ranks of European civilization of the time. They were little more as yet than children of nature, and in consequence it is essential not to omit the consideration of any single factor which may have influenced their actions. Beyond the call of nature's necessity, there is for such a people only one other stimulus, if such it may be called, and that is, as Tacitus said of their choice of a habitation, the prompting of their own sweet will.

CHAPTER II

Methods of Study and History of Anglo-Saxon Archaeological Research

The second method by which some light can be thrown on the obscurity of this period of English history is by a careful study of the objects found in the graves. In the last chapter it was assumed that the graves in question were those of Anglo-Saxons, and of the earliest period. It might seem superfluous to refer to such an assumption at all, but, as the writer once had the question put to him, ' But how do you know they are Anglo-Saxon ? ', it is perhaps only right that all doubt on that score should be removed. In the first place, the graves containing the relics usually known as Anglo-Saxon are only found within the limits of the districts which history designates as the scene of the early activities of that race. Thus in Cornwall and Devon, and even nearer eastwards in Dorset, no such graves have come to light, nor are they found in what are recognized as other Celt-inhabited parts, such as Wales, the counties along the western coast of England, north of the Mersey, nor finally in Scotland or Ireland. It is in the Eastern Counties and the Midlands that these graves are found in the greatest numbers. That they cannot have been dug nor the objects found in them deposited therein before the end of the fourth or beginning of the fifth century of our era at earliest is proved by the not unusual discovery of late fourth-century Roman coins. In addition, other objects of the latest period of Roman occupation, whose date is vouchsafed by similar well-authenticated finds on the Continent, are found in association with relics of types which never appear in purely Roman graves. Further, in cases of inhuma-

tion, examination of the skull-types has shown that the
people who buried their dead with such relics belonged to a
type never found in England in Roman or pre-Roman times,
but, on the other hand, to one which is of common occurrence
in North Germany; in short, to the districts from which tradition brought the ancestors of the English race. These
are but a few of the arguments for assigning the contents of
these graves to the Teutonic invaders. On the question of
the exact limits of time within which they must be placed,
further evidence can be obtained from a careful correlation of
associated finds. It is only within recent years that the
scientific methods which have been employed with such
success in other fields of archaeological research, have been
brought to bear upon the mass of material recovered in the
past from Anglo-Saxon graves. It has already been pointed
out that this material carries with it an especial value in view
of the shortness of the period to which it must be assigned, and
it is certain that a continued application of methodical comparison and correlation—for there is room still for a great deal
of work in this field—will lead to important results in showing
the relative value of archaeology in the reconstruction of early
Anglo-Saxon history, which has hitherto depended mainly on
the researches of the historian, philologist, and the student
of social institutions. From a correlation of associated finds
some idea can be obtained of the dates at which any given
cemetery first began to be used and at which it fell into
disuse. In some localities it renders it possible to surmise an
initial occupation by one tribe and its eventual dispossession
by members of another, owing to the variation in the types of
objects used for similar purposes among the different racial
elements of which the immigrating Teutons were composed.
In view of the comparatively small area which was at first
occupied by the invaders, this divergence of types is far more
strongly marked than on the Continent for an area of far
greater extent. And it is this very extensiveness of the
Continental regions over which either exactly similar objects
or their prototypes are diffused, which makes the comparative

study of the English relics of such importance. Were it possible to find the extraordinary variety of types which appear in England, within an area of equal extent on the Continent, the problems connected with the origin of the invaders and the districts occupied by them in this country would be comparatively simple. It is this conjunction of limitation and divergence which lends to the study of early Anglo-Saxon archaeology a fascination hardly surpassed by that of any other period.

The difficulty resulting from these features is one which affects the questions of Anglo-Saxon archaeology as a whole, but there are others to be considered which relate more particularly to the study of the relics obtained from the graves. They are—

(i) the existence of two alternative methods of disposing of the dead, namely inhumation and cremation. This is perhaps the most disturbing factor which has to be reckoned with. It has often been stated in the past that cremation was characteristic of the Anglian cemeteries, inhumation of Saxon and Jutish graves. As a general statement of fact this is roughly speaking correct, but the diffusion of these two methods cannot be explained in so simple a manner. There are so many exceptions and anomalies, certainly within the districts assigned to the Anglian and Saxon elements, that to dismiss the question with such a generality is to shirk one of the most difficult points in the whole of Anglo-Saxon archaeology. Professor Chadwick has touched on this point in *The Origin of the English Nation*, and has well recognized some of the difficulties, but he is unfortunately under a misconception about the meaning of the instances of cremation found in the Jutish and adjacent districts. These examples cannot be considered apart from the relics which have in most cases been found with interments in the same cemeteries.[2] The most serious obstacle to a straightforward assignment of the different rites to one or other element of the invaders will be recognized when their origin from an archaeological standpoint is

[1] p. 73.   [2] See *infra*, p. 115.

discussed in subsequent chapters. It will be found that the diffusion of the variant rites on the Continent is almost the exact inverse to what is the case in England, a fact which imports another question into the whole problem, namely, to what extent the Anglian and Saxon tribes, at any rate, changed their methods of disposal of the dead after their arrival in this country, at what period they did so, and how long the two rites existed concurrently. That the first of these queries may be answered in the affirmative is absolutely certain; as will appear in a marked degree in the case of Wessex. The period at which the change occurred is inseparable from a comparative examination of the antiquities and must be left therefore until the relics obtained from the different parts of England are considered in detail. With regard to the last point it may be said at once that there is good evidence that the practice of cremation, which as might naturally be expected was the one to call forth the most vehement protests from the Christian missionaries, survived right down to the latest period for which archaeological material is available. The attitude of the Church towards this rite was a very hostile one, and is nowhere better exemplified than in the 8th Capitulary of Charlemagne, which enacted capital punishment on 'any one who shall have caused the corpse of a deceased person to be consumed by fire according to the rite of the heathen and shall have reduced the bones to ashes'.

(ii) The second difficulty arises from the fact that in some districts the grave furniture was less rich and varied than in others. It is sometimes difficult to find a sufficient number of graves containing more than one distinctive type of object, so that the deductions which can be drawn from a correlation of types in the various districts are somewhat unequal. These inequalities will, however, probably tend to disappear with the greatly improved methods which have come into being in recent years, in the excavating of the graves and the recording of their contents.

(iii) Lastly there arises the question of the orientation of graves as evidence of an earlier or later period in the history of the early settlements. Probably one of the most dangerous assumptions which can be made in reference to Anglo-Saxon burials is that, when in a given grave the deceased person was laid with his head to the West and his feet to the East, it may be taken as a sign that Christian beliefs were beginning to make themselves felt among the inhabitants. In some cemeteries where a large number of graves with promiscuous orientation are found alongside of others orientated in the Christian manner, there may be much to be said for this hypothesis, provided that it can be shown that the earliest types of objects are always associated with promiscuous orientation, the commonest form of which is the disposition of the deceased with the head to the South-West. As a matter of fact, it can be clearly proved that this rule never holds good, though it may not be very apparent in every case ; on the other hand it can be equally clearly demonstrated that in one area at least the so-called Christian orientation is nothing of the sort, as it is practically universal and was in use from the period of the first settlements. Its existence in that area may conceivably be attributed to influences at work on the settlers prior to their immigrations, but there is nothing to show that they were anything but pagans at the time of their arrival in England.

In addition to the correlation of associated types, which is perhaps the soundest method available for comparative dating, a large amount of useful information can be obtained from the purely typological method. By taking a large series of objects of one particular type, it is possible to obtain some general conclusions as to the evolutionary process by which the particular type was developed. Two considerations have to be borne in mind in using this method as a criterion for purposes of dating, firstly that of mere form, and secondly that of decoration. The former is in a large measure self-evident, if the series of objects which can be brought together is sufficiently extensive to furnish all the links in the chain of development ; the latter, however, is wrapped up in the history of the art-motives in vogue during the period which is covered

by the objects thus decorated.   In the first case the material
available for study in early Anglo-Saxon times is in the nature
of the case somewhat limited, for, if such material is only to
be obtained from the contents of graves, it is evident that
there cannot be any very great variety of types.   The graves
of Anglo-Saxon men are not of much service for this purpose,
as the relics deposited with even the more richly equipped
warrior show no great variety throughout the whole period.
The usual objects associated with such graves are the spear,
the shield (represented by the iron boss), a knife, and the
furnishings of the belt ; the presence of a sword seems to denote
a person of higher rank ; others may be equipped with the
long dirk, the 'seax'; occasionally, also, accessory vessels
of pottery, wood, bronze, or glass are found.   From all these,
with the exception perhaps of the belt-fittings, not much
information can be gained.   Certain forms of buckles are of
earlier or later date, and in a few instances the evidence of form
is supported by decoration.   But no perceptible change is to
be noted in the shape of the weapons ; only the shield-bosses,
the form of which varies considerably, may throw some light
on the particular part of the Continent from which their
owners were sprung.   Far more reliable and definite information
is furnished by the contents of the graves of women.   Even in
these early times the subservience of the feminine mind to the
dictates of fashion is clearly perceptible, more especially in
that most distinctive article of feminine attire—even far back
in prehistoric times—the *fibula* or brooch.   Even within the
short period under inquiry this one object alone was subjected
to most radical alteration and development, sometimes in the
form, sometimes in the decoration.   Further, the evidence
supplied by the women's graves proves the tribal instinct to
have been at first immensely strong, and the diffusion of the
various types should receive full consideration before the
conclusions of history or the like are accepted as final.

To turn to the second consideration, namely that of the
decorative motives employed by the early Anglo-Saxons, it is
self-evident that no proper estimate of them can be obtained

apart from a knowledge of the contemporary or slightly earlier art of the remainder of the Germanic races on the Continent. There, the history of this art is inseparably bound up with that of 'the Migrations', and in the same way as it is possible to differentiate two main lines of migration westwards, the one northern and the other southern, similarly, two corresponding art-provinces may be distinguished. Naturally a considerable overlap is observable within those regions lying between the two extremities, more especially when the two streams of migration are seen to impinge upon one another. Owing to the fact, however, that in addition to the westward movement there was a flow of northern tribes like the Burgunds and Langobards southwards, an appreciable diffusion of northern art-motives is to be observed in central and southern Europe, while the art of northern Europe remained comparatively pure. The origins of this latter art are somewhat obscure, but most generally accepted opinion is that it represents the Germanic expression of ideas derived from late provincial Roman sources. An attempt has even been made to attribute the initial stages entirely to the classical art-world, but in view of the distribution of the motives which constitute the background of this art, it is doubtful whether such an attempt can be regarded as successful.[1] It makes its first appearance just in those districts where the Teutonic tribes and the Roman Empire came into full conflict, and exactly at the period when the Roman power was beginning to give way before the insistent pressure of its Germanic adversaries. The motives employed in this northern art-province may be divided into two classes, the first consisting of purely geometric designs, or of designs geometric in character but derived originally from motives belonging to the plant-world. The roots of this class of motives indubitably lie in the last representatives of classical art-production in the Roman provinces along the line of the *limes*, while it still remained unbroken by invading hordes of the barbarians. The second class is composed of

---

[1] A. Riegl, *Spätrömische Kunstindustrie.*

a system of zoomorphic patterns, the main origin of which has been thought to be a particular form of crouching animal often associated with the earliest stages of the geometric class above mentioned (fig. 2). The problem has attracted the attention of several northern archaeologists, among whom Sophus Müller, Söderberg, and Salin deserve particular mention. The first-named regards it as purely Germanic both in origin and conception, while the last two favour the influences from the Roman world. Be that as it may, it is certain that nothing but the mere impetus came from that side, and that the credit for its whole evolution must be assigned to the Germans and to them alone.

The geometric class of design comprises certain important subdivisions, due partly to the design itself and partly to the method of execution. The interdependence of design and method are illustrated in a remarkable manner by the purely geometric patterns employed on many metal objects. They are executed according to a technique derived from wood-carving, usually known by the German title of 'Kerbschnitt' or chip-carving (see fig. 2). The application of this method demonstrates more than almost anything else the Germanic feeling lying at the back of the designs thus executed, for the technique is quite foreign to classical art as a whole, while it is on all fours with the employment of timber for architectural purposes among the Teutonic tribes, to which reference has been made in the first chapter. This 'negative'—to give it the epithet used by Salin—expression of design is used alike for geometric patterns composed of straight lines, spirals, stars, and the like, and when applied to metal-work produces a contrast of light and shade which is by no means brought out so effectively by the employment of the alternative method, namely of relief against a flat background, or, as Salin terms it, the 'positive' method. This is the technique which is most commonly used in reproducing such patterns, often geometric in appearance, as are derived from the classical acanthus and similar motives. In the North, designs based on such patterns are of the simplest character, and are practically confined to a tendril-design which almost certainly owes its origin to the trails of the classical acanthus-motive, rather than to the spiral proper, which is found in Northern art as far back as the Bronze Age at least. The geometric patterns belong as a whole to the earliest period of Germanic art, and in the South are found surviving in one form or another right down to the time when they were incorporated in the classical

FIG. 2. BRONZE ORNAMENTAL PLATE WITH COMBINATION OF 'KERBSCHNITT' AND ZOOMORPHIC DECORATION.

renaissance of Carolingian times. But in the North they were gradually forced to give place to the more distinctive form of Teutonic ornament, namely the zoomorphic. This class of ornament can be best studied from objects discovered in Scandinavia and Denmark, where it flourished for close on five hundred years, passing through several stages of evolution. A full account of these stages can be found in Salin's work *Die Altgermanische Thierornamentik*, but it may be advantageous to give a short *résumé* here, as some knowledge of the lines along which this system of ornament developed, is essential in dealing with questions of comparative dating of Anglo-Saxon relics. The problem of the origin of this ornament has already been touched upon; it merely remains to say that in the earliest stages the animal forms are reproduced in relief in a fairly naturalistic manner and without the use of any schematic artifice for emphasizing any particular feature. Quite soon, however, there begin to creep in indications which demonstrate that this zoomorphic art was in the main that of the mere craftsman copying from set designs or modifying them to suit his immediate purpose, rather than that of the artist working from nature. This comes out in the practice of outlining the relief form with contour-lines, and it is these contour-lines which eventually gain predominance to the exclusion of almost every other part of the design. The process of copying, as always happens, led moreover to the production of many examples exhibiting a total lack of understanding of the nature of the design, and this, coupled with the existence of a *horror vacui*, such as is found in most barbaric systems of art, eventually caused a decadence to set in. During this period of decadence it would be often wellnigh impossible to realize what lay at the back of many of the designs, were it not that the chain of evolution places it beyond a doubt that what look at first sight like meaningless lines in reality represent one or more parts of a schematic animal form (fig. 3). The more capable craftsmen, however, succeeded in evolving a further system in which full advantage was taken of the fact that the form of the animal was now entirely designated by contour-lines. The idea at the back of these they thought well to totally ignore, and thus, as it were, a new style came into existence which was characterized by designs in which the contour-lines of one or more animals were entwined and interlaced to form a definite pattern, such as may be found in the illuminated manuscripts of Ireland and elsewhere. In the North this change can on various grounds be dated to the latter part of the sixth century. Taking it as his basis, Salin has formulated a system of 'Styles' in this

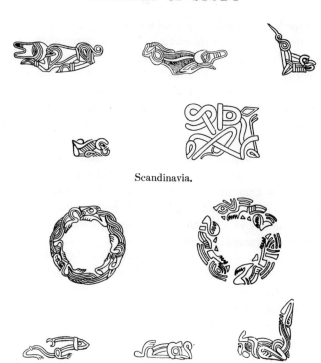

Scandinavia.

England.
Zoomorphic Ornament, *c.* 450–600.

Europe.

England.
Zoomorphic Ornament, *c.* 600–700.

Fig. 3. Examples of Zoomorphic Ornament.

zoomorphic art, of which the first covers the last half of the fifth and the whole of the sixth century, while the second Style includes the seventh century. The change already noted is accompanied by others which consist in the nature of innovations of certain details, as in the configuration of the animal's head and limbs. These are all of a very marked character, and taken in conjunction with the form of the object to which the decoration is applied provide an approximate date which can often be corroborated by outside evidence. No account is taken here of the development of zoomorphic ornament beyond the seventh century, as it has no bearing on the problems of early Anglo-Saxon archaeology. It is not unknown in Central and Southern Europe, whither it was doubtless carried by the Langobards and other northern tribes moving southwards, and where it is not appreciably later in time. The lines of its development there also resemble what has been observed in the north; the differences are merely such as might be looked for in any widely separated localities, but in the south the influence of plait-work and similar motives seems to have been early at work. It only remains to add a few general remarks on the occurrence of this northern zoomorphic art in England. The approximate limits of time within which the pagan cemeteries were in use, naturally restrict the examples of this art available for study to such as might have been made before the middle of the seventh century, and as some time would be needed for the spread of any innovations, the different styles would make their first appearance in this country at a somewhat later date than on the Continent. The result is that examples executed according to the canons of Style II are quite rare except in Kent, which being in more ways than one accessible to influence from the Frankish culture, would likely enough have acquired some knowledge of the changes evolved by Continental craftsmen. That Kent must have been the medium through which any such knowledge infiltrated into England is corroborated by the evidence obtainable from philological and literary research.

These, negatively supported by absence of historical records
to the contrary, seem to prove that all intercourse between
the Anglo-Saxons and their kinsmen in Northern Europe
must have ceased soon after the middle of the sixth century.
So far as England outside of Kent is concerned, the historical
coincides roughly with the artistic evidence, as an examination of existing examples shows that there Salin's Style I
held its own throughout.   It reaches such a pitch of
decadence that, without the early specimens to serve as
a guide, the later productions would be absolutely unintel-
ligible.   Constant repetition brought with it the inevitable
results, and many of the latest examples of this ornamentation prior to the conversion of England to Christianity recall
to some extent the simple linear designs of the earliest period,
but they lack the grace and harmony which are often pos-
sessed by the latter.

The Continental races which lay along the line of the
southern stream of migration were not dependent to the same
extent on one method of decoration, as was the case in the
north.   The Gothic tribes, when they swarmed over the
Roman Empire in the fifth century, brought with them
a technique which must be regarded as one of the most
attractive in the whole of early Teutonic art.   This is
the use of garnets and other semi-precious stones, set in
cloisons to decorate jewellery and the like.   It is a technique
which is hardly known in the north during this early period,
and its non-appearance there has an important bearing on
the question of the origin of a part of the invaders of
England.   The contrast of colour produced by this method,
particularly in examples in which garnets were arranged in
a pattern in gold cloison settings interspersed with stones or
glass of other colours, was wholly in accordance with the
semi-barbaric tastes of a race who, if not actually akin to, had
at least lived at one time in close contact with Asiatic peoples
among whom this style of art was especially favoured.   The
technical skill which produced many of the objects thus
ornamented, both on the Continent and in England, must

have been of a very high order, and it must be admitted that for appreciation of colour effects and harmony of design the Kentish craftsmen of the end of the pagan period yield in nothing to their Continental contemporaries.

Finally there is the question how far this Teutonic art was affected in England by Roman survivals. This is a difficult point upon which to offer any very definite opinion, as the presence, in the early Continental art of the period, of motives obtained from classical sources has already been noted, and the comparative isolation of England as an art-province may account for their apparent survival to a time when they had elsewhere been consigned to the limbo of unfashionable antiquity. At the same time, this very isolation may have caused the Anglo-Saxon craftsmen to restock their repertory from time to time from the store of such motives as were immediately available, and in spite of the havoc which followed the withdrawal of Rome, there is little reason to imagine that every sign or trace of classical art had entirely vanished off the face of England. It is only necessary to call to mind the first Anglo-Saxon coinage, the sceattas, the earliest of which belong to about A.D. 600, to realize that the Anglo-Saxons were prone to seek inspiration among the relics of Roman Britain.

For the study of Anglo-Saxon art, England may be divided into four provinces. Two of these seem to coincide with the districts assigned by Bede to the tribes of the Jutes and Saxons, but various considerations which will be dealt with in detail at a later stage seem to call for the division of the region occupied by his Angles into two provinces, one of which may still be called Anglian, while the other, presenting an admixture of Anglian and Saxon features, may be suitably termed Anglo-Saxon (fig. 4). The accompanying map also includes for purposes of reference the boundaries of the early kingdoms as accepted by historical writers.

Before turning to a contemplation of the archaeological material which these provinces have produced, it may be permissible to give a brief account of the work that has been done in the past in this branch of archaeological research. Almost instinctively the mind turns first to that delightful work, the *Hydriotaphia* of Sir Thomas Browne. No more charming preface to any branch of archaeological study has ever been written than this description of 'sad sepulchral pitchers' which were no other than Anglian cinerary urns unearthed at Walsingham in Norfolk. Sir Thomas Browne, indeed, assigned them to the Romans, but in that he only acted in consonance with all antiquaries of his own time as well as those of more than a century later. To them every antiquity which could not be dated by comparison with remains actually existing above ground, or authenticated by historical records, whether it were a neolithic celt, a bronze palstave, or a Late Celtic urn, were one and all attributed to the race whom the revival of classical learning had endowed with a new importance by reason of the Latin works describing the events connected with the Roman occupation. Possibly the earliest Anglo-Saxon relic existing in any English collection may have been one of the urns so vividly described in the *Hydriotaphia*. Among the objects comprising what remains of the original collections in the Ashmolean Museum is an urn of this type which there is good reason to suppose once was included in the 'closet of rarities' at Lambeth known as 'Tradescant's Ark'. In the Catalogue published by John Tradescant the younger in 1656, the following entry '2 Roman Urnes' occurs.[1] This agrees in part with one in the first catalogue of such objects made after the donation of the Tradescant Collections to the University of Oxford by Elias Ashmole in 1683. In this manuscript catalogue, compiled by a famous antiquary of his day, Edward Lhwyd, first assistant-keeper under Dr. Robert Plot and later second keeper, it runs as follows: 'Three other Roman urns, large, having protuberant bellies . . .'[2]

[1] *Musaeum Tradescantianum*, p. 44.

[2] The Catalogue is written in the quaint Latin of the day. '683. *Tres aliae urnae Romanae, magnae, ventres habent protuberantes, quarum una in collum terminatur, viminibus circundatur; alterae duae collis carent.*' The urn in question still bears its original paper number.

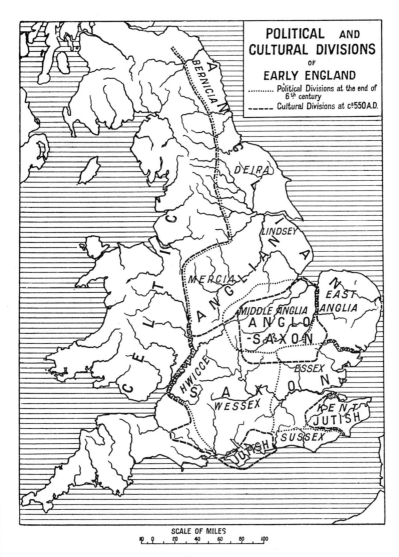

FIG. 4.

The fame which the Tradescant collections enjoyed at the
time, and also the well-known fact that the sources from
which the contents of those collections, especially of the
cabinet of curiosities as apart from objects illustrating
natural history, included notable persons of the times, suggest
that Sir Thomas Browne may have been among these latter,
and that to the urns which John Tradescant included in his
catalogue, yet another was added by the author of the
Hydriotaphia. It was not, however, until the latter part
of the eighteenth century that any scientific examination of
Anglo-Saxon graves was carried out, when the Rev. Bryan
Faussett conducted an extensive series of excavations between
the years 1757–1773 among the cemeteries of Kent, and
brought together the magnificent collections now in the
Liverpool Museum. His manuscript account of his finds,
edited by Roach Smith in 1856, under the title of *Inventorium Sepulchrale*, is a model of accurate recording based on
careful and methodical excavation. Faussett failed, however,
to realize the true significance of his discoveries; like his
predecessors he assigned them to the Romans ; and the credit
for first recognizing these remains as Anglo-Saxon belongs to
the Rev. James Douglas, who from 1779 onwards excavated
a series of graves on the site of Chatham Lines, the contents
of which he subsequently described in *Nenia Britannica*.
A part of his collections was given in 1829 to Oxford by
Sir Richard Colt-Hoare, who himself recovered a small
number of Saxon relics from Wiltshire tumuli. The
beginning of the latter half of last century witnessed several
important excavations, and notable writings on the subject by
antiquaries of the day, among whom Akerman, Roach Smith,
Kemble, and Wylie call for particular mention. Since that
time hardly a year has passed without the discovery of some
cemetery or isolated relics in some part of the territory
occupied by the invaders; to recent critical study of the
material reference has already been made in the Preface.

It has been usual in the past, in treating of the different
provinces into which Anglo-Saxon relics are divided, to take

Fig. 5.   Urn from the Tradescant Collection.

them in the order in which, according to history, these provinces or districts were settled, that is to say, Jutish, Saxon, and Anglian, but in the present work it has been deemed advisable to leave the description of the Jutish culture until last, as without first obtaining a knowledge of the other districts, it seems impossible to arrive at a full appreciation of the problems which surround the distinctive culture of the area which the Jutes are said to have occupied.

CHAPTER III

THE SAXONS

In Bede's day, it is evident from his remarks that a tri-
partite division of the Saxon tribes was generally recognized,
namely the East, South, and West Saxons. How far this division is original, and how far it was the outcome of growth of
tribal areas owning allegiance to separate ruling houses, and
as such later than the beginning of the invasions, it would be
difficult to say. There is certainly something artificial in such
a division, and yet as two of the divisions at least figure
prominently in the earliest records as political entities, it may
be assumed that all three came into existence at a very early
period, in the first instance doubtless under pressure of the
need for combination against a common foe. It is equally
certain, however, that in the end their continuance was more
than a little due to their geographical position. If, as the
names of the three districts suggest, the tribes or septs which
settled in them were sprung from a common stock, it is only
natural to expect that their culture would be of a similar
character with occasional local variations, and so far as the
South and West Saxons are concerned, this is certainly the
case ; the evidence with regard to Essex, or the East Saxons,
is not so clear. Mention is made by the earliest writers of
Middle Saxons, but no kingdom or petty chieftainship
occupying an area designated by the name Middlesex is
known. Situated between the East and West Saxons, it plays
no striking part in the early events, again partly for geographical reasons, but also possibly on account of the survival
of London as a corporate community in its midst. Any
connexions it may have had with one or other of the two main

districts seem to incline rather to the side of Wessex, a point which may be left until that area comes under consideration.

A. *East Saxons.*

Taking the three districts separately in their geographical order from East to West, Essex from the side of archaeology proves extraordinarily disappointing. Considering the position it occupies in relation to the Continent and the enormous importance of Colchester in Roman times, it might naturally be expected that this county would have yielded a corresponding wealth of antiquities as evidence of a considerable settlement. Professor Chadwick [1] concludes from the traditional genealogy of its ruling house that the East Saxons came of different stock to the others but that they were almost certainly Saxons, and archaeology to some extent confirms this, but it is very doubtful whether he is right in surmising that Essex was the most populous of the three Saxon kingdoms, or that its rulers were usually supreme over the other two. The latter statement would require historical evidence to support it, and such does not exist ; while the former is corroborated neither by what little is known of its early history nor by archaeology.

Hemmed in by the powerful and populous Anglian tribes to the north, the River Thames to the south with the still more powerful Kentish kingdom on its opposite bank, and the forests of Hainault and Epping to the west, it would be strange if in the early days, when the different tribes were as ready to spring at one another's throats as at those of their British adversaries, this district had been able to acquire anything like a predominating influence over its neighbours. It has also to be remembered that a large part of the county is covered by heavy clay soils ; the London Clay formation accounts for nearly a third of its surface, and it may be accepted as a working guide to exploration in the field, that areas of clay land were carefully avoided by the earliest settlers. Exceptions do occur, as even at Shoebury where burials have

[1] Op. cit., pp. 88, 89.

been found, but such finds more often than not represent temporary cemeteries, of a time when the invaders had not yet made their foothold secure. As will be seen from the map (fig. 1) the settlements vouched for by cemeteries are with two exceptions all in the northern part of the county; situated chiefly along the rivers Blackwater and Colne. The principal ones are at Kelvedon, Marks Tey, and Feering, but none of them has yielded much material for study. The relics are as a whole unimportant, and in some respects not sufficiently distinctive to admit of definite assignment either to a Saxon population or to an influx of settlers from a more northerly part of the Continent. One point in favour of the Saxons is the absence of authenticated cases of cremation. This, however, in itself would not be conclusive, as cremation is not exclusively an Anglian trait. The position of Colchester after the conquest is one of the chief problems on which more light would be welcome. It has been pointed out that the Roman name Colonia castra is faithfully carried on in the Saxon title, Colneceaster, but such also is the case with a large number of similar place-names throughout England; the mere survival of the name does not imply occupation by the invaders. There must have been a Saxon community of some kind in the vicinity, as some objects have been found near the town, but it does not seem to have been of any size. The history of Essex towards the close of the pagan period is closely bound up with that of Kent, whose vassals the Essex rulers appear to have become; in consequence, evidences of influence from that quarter are not wanting. The most striking instance is the rich grave found at Broomfield; where, along with a sword, spear-head, shield-boss, bronze-bound cups, iron-bound buckets, an iron cauldron and a curious iron cup, were also found studs and part of a buckle with cloison decoration, a bronze-handled pan and glass vases all strongly suggesting close intercourse with Kent, and lastly a wheel-made vase which can be exactly paralleled from the same county. The survival of a Romano-British population in the interior and a preponderance of the Anglo-Saxon type on the

coast, which Beddoe has deduced from his observation of
existing physical types, receive therefore some support from
the archaeology of this early period, as also does the kinship
of the modern Essex dialect to that of Kent, and its divergence
from the speech of East Anglia north of the Stour.

B.   *South Saxons.*

A particular interest attaches itself to Sussex, as it is the
first Saxon kingdom to which history makes any reference.
Its beginnings, traditionally connected with Ælla and the year
477, date well back into the fifth century, and twenty years
before the West Saxons are said to have set foot in the West.
Owing to its position, hemmed in as it was by the marshland
on the Kentish border and the dense forest of the Andredes-
weald stretching the whole length of its northern frontier, it
is generally considered to have passed an almost isolated existence, practically unaffected by its neighbours until the seventh
century, when it came under the sway of the more powerful tribe
of the West Saxons.   The situation of its cemeteries along
a narrow strip of coastal land between Pevensey and Bognor,
and bounded by the Weald on the north, would certainly
suggest that this isolation was real, and, roughly speaking,
the antiquities which these cemeteries have yielded prove that
the South Saxon kingdom was not greatly affected by influences
from the surrounding districts.   It is, on the other hand,
a question whether Sussex did not itself exert some influence
on at least one of its neighbours, as dimly indicated in the
tradition that Ælla was the first Anglo-Saxon ruler who
exercised a hegemony over England.   Such traditions as
these are vague in the extreme and often of very doubtful
value, but this is due to the insufficiency of the records of
early Anglo-Saxon history as a whole, and they are not
necessarily more than exaggerations, which there is no absolute
means of refuting.   A study of the Sussex relics of the period
seems to offer proof that the tradition of Ælla's hegemony at
least contains a kernel of truth.   The cemeteries known as
yet are not numerous, and only three are of any size, namely

High Down near Ferring, Saxonbury near Kingston, and finally
Alfriston. Most of them are situated within the somewhat
constricted area between the Cuckmere and the Ouse. Far
the greater proportion of the interments are by inhumation ;
cremation up to the present is unknown at Alfriston, and at
High Down, along with eighty-six interments, there occurred
only ten cases of cremation. The result is in some respects
a gain to archaeology, as cremation urns in England contain
as a rule nothing of importance. The culture displayed by
the finds in these cemeteries is, except for a few importations,
purely Saxon in character, and its most outstanding features
are best illustrated by the relics from the graves of women.
Many of these are richly furnished, but until the accounts of
the recent excavations at Alfriston are published in full, any
deductions based on a comparison of associated finds must be
deferred. It is in the general character of the relics, their
types and ornamentation, that the chief interest lies. The
two cemeteries of High Down and Alfriston have yielded
what seems at first sight to be an extraordinary number of
saucer brooches, when it is remembered that by writers in the
middle of the late century this type is usually spoken of as
West Saxon, and as restricted to the West Saxon districts,
a conclusion even then based on an imperfect knowledge of
the material. One of the most difficult points in connexion
with the type is the question of its origin, and even though
this still remain unsettled for some time to come, it seems
that the recent finds at Alfriston, taken in conjunction with
those at High Down, throw some light on the problem as to
where they first came into general use in South England, and
consequently who were the agents for their diffusion. The
answer should be Sussex, and the reason for giving that Saxon
kingdom the credit for the wide-spread distribution of this
type of brooch lies in the limited style of ornamentation.
Out of 33 examples on which the pattern is visible, no less
than 27 are decorated with geometric patterns, and, what is
more important, these show careful execution. The predominance of such designs points to an early immigration before

the Teutonic zoomorphic motives had had time to wholly capture the artistic tastes of the South Saxons, but the point which calls for special attention is that within the collections from the three cemeteries occurs an assemblage of patterns, some very distinctive in character, which are only found scattered at different places within the West Saxon sphere of influence, such as Horton Kirby and Northfleet (Kent),[1] Croydon and Mitcham (Surrey), Droxford (Hants), and numerous cemeteries in Berkshire and Oxfordshire. The commonest of these designs is a running pattern of five or six spirals, but more important for chronology are others in which the gradual subjection of geometric to zoomorphic motives can be traced. Two of these are given in the accompanying figure (fig. 6). The Roman piece (a) from Bowcombe Down, Isle of Wight, shows the initial stage of one. Round the edge also is a degraded repetition of a motive commonly found on late-Roman knife-handles (many known from Kentish graves of the Anglo-Saxon period), namely a dog chasing a hare.[2] In (b) the introduction of the favourite Teutonic face-motive comes out. Both this and the transitional stage in which the motive is adopted in its original state by the Saxons are represented in South Saxon finds. The other design is even more interesting. In (d) remains of the common Roman looped design (c) appears, within an ovule border. This is taken from a saucer brooch found distorted by heat in a cremation urn at High Down. The combination of the design and the cremation burial argues for an early date on account of the scarcity of cremation within this district (see *infra*, p. 58). The transformation which the design underwent at the hands of Saxon craftsmen is well shown by the third example figured (e), where the arms of the rhomboid have become the legs of the Teutonic decorative animal. A stage in which the rhomboidal character of the design is better preserved has been recently found at Alfriston. Quite a large number of other finds, whose

---

[1] For the apparent anomaly presented by the inclusion of Kentish cemeteries an explanation will be found below, p. 115.

[2] e. g. *Arch. Cantiana*, x. 307.

diffusion can hardly be attributed entirely to chance, serves to link together the South and West Saxon cultures.[1] They may denote nothing more than a common origin, but taken in connexion with the tradition of Ælla's hegemony they are at least suggestive, even if it is difficult to understand the existence of a lively intercourse between the Sussex coast and the Thames Valley, separated as they were from one another by

FIG. 6. APPLICATION OF ROMAN MOTIVES IN SAXON ART.

the thick forest of the Weald. The main Roman road, which ran northwards from Chichester to London, may or may not have been used by the Saxons, and in any case it is doubtful whether the theory of the isolation of Sussex is entirely correct. Some traces of intercourse with Jutish tribes, possibly more with the Isle of Wight and the Jutish settlements in Hampshire

[1] Contrast on this point Chadwick, *Origin of the English Nation*, pp. 34 and 87, with Hoops' *Reallexikon der germanischen Altertumskunde*, article on *Englisches Siedelungswesen*, p. 602.

than with Kent, can be seen among the Sussex relics (see also *infra*, p. 118). One little trait in these relics is perhaps distinctive of Sussex alone. It is to be seen in broad annular or penannular brooches, which are provided with stops on either side of the slot through which the pin passes, to prevent its coming unfastened. This brooch-type is also represented by ornate examples, on which a tendril pattern is associated

FIG. 7. PENANNULAR BROOCH FROM SARRE, KENT.

with a peculiar form of zoomorphic design found on other Sussex objects. One of these brooches found in Kent (fig. 7)[1] probably emanated from a Sussex workshop.

C. *West Saxons*

The earliest activities of the West Saxons are, thanks to the writings of the early chroniclers, inseparably associated with the part of the south coast which lies opposite the

[1] *V. C. H., Kent*, i. 361, fig. 12.

Isle of Wight. The legends connected with the names of
Cerdic and his sons have served as the groundwork on which
every account of the West Saxons has been based, but they
have been subjected to much criticism, chiefly on account of
the un-Saxon form of the name of Cerdic and its close
similarity to the Welsh Caradoc, as well as of the curious
regularity in the intervals of time which separate the records
of different events. Whatever may be the value of such
criticism, it is certain that archaeology finds itself in sharp
antagonism to the traditional accounts, and for that reason
the events may be briefly stated here. The landing-place
of the West Saxons in 495 is given as Cerdicesore, the site of
which is unknown, and again in 504 at Porta, which name is
suggestive of the modern Portsmouth. The modern town,
however, is situated in the territory which Bede allots to a
branch of the Jutes who—to judge from the further statement
that in 530 Cerdic overran the Isle of Wight, also a Jutish
district, and after subduing it, handed it over to Stuf and
Withgar—must have already been in occupation of the Isle of
Wight before the arrival of the West Saxons. It is therefore
difficult to conceive that the latter would have chosen to
disembark in what must have been hostile territory. It is,
however, usual to place the scene of the landing in Southampton Water, on account of the occurrence of a battle at
Natanleod, identified with Netley, in 508. The next event of
importance is a battle at Cerdicesford (? Charford on the
Dorset Avon) in 519. To the period between that date and
the capture of Saerobyrig in 552 is usually assigned the
series of battles linked with the name of Arthur, culminating
in the fight at Mons Badonicus. After 552 a further four
years elapsed, to be followed by the battle of Beranbyrig in
556, the site of which is now generally held to be Barbury
Rings on the Marlborough Downs. This carries the history
of the West Saxons down to the middle of the sixth century,
and then and not till then do they appear in history in the
Thames valley, the first operation recorded in that area being
the defeat of Æthelbert at Wibbandune (? Wimbledon) in

568. The whole history of the West Saxons down to this point is consequently one of constant struggles to obtain a mastery of Hampshire and Wiltshire, and it is hard to understand how any extensive settlements could have been established so long as their position was so precarious as the traditions would suggest. Had the process of occupation been wholly effected from the south coast, it would naturally be expected that more than a few cemeteries would have been discovered to bear witness to it. But what are the actual facts ? In the whole of Hampshire outside the Jutish district, not a single cemetery is known. An isolated find at Woolbury up the Itchen valley and a few weapons found at Winchester are all that is forthcoming to prove that the Teutonic invaders were ever in this part of the country at all.[1] The Winchester discovery helps little, as owing to the proximity of this city to the Jutes, it is more likely that its fall is to be credited to that race, if it did not occur in some earlier piratical raid shortly after the withdrawal of the Legions. The Woolbury objects are too scanty to serve as a basis for any very definite conclusions ; all that can be said is that they are Saxon in character. Doubtless the dense forests of Hampshire deterred the Saxons from attempting much, and were it not for the traditions, there would be almost no reason to imagine that they set foot in that county until a much later period. The legend—it is no more than that—of the burial of Cerdic at Winchester seems only to be an attempt to put the final resting-place of the first West Saxon monarch in the city which afterwards became the capital of the kingdom, and for a time even of England itself. In Wiltshire things are not very much better. Cemeteries are, it is true, not unknown, and one of them at Harnham Hill, near Salisbury, is fairly large. A smaller one was found in 1822 at Bassett Down, a little north-west of Marlborough. Other graves have been brought to light

---

[1] The statement made by the writer in *Archaeologia*, lxiii, p. 164, that Saxon cinerary urns had been found at Christchurch, Hants, now appears to have been based on a misunderstanding.

round Devizes and in the Wyley Valley, and in many of the
Bronze Age barrows which occur in such numbers on Salisbury Plain and other parts of the Downs. Among the relics
recovered from the graves in the two cemeteries, there is
nothing to which anything like an early date can be assigned,
in fact nothing that could not well have been deposited there
at or about the time at which the events recorded by the
Chronicle are placed. The burials in barrows of a more
ancient period are practically always those of men, and thus
suggest nothing more than warriors who fell in the many
conflicts with the British. The fine jewellery associated with
an interment in a coffin in a barrow on Roundway Down, near
Devizes, is more than probably of late date; the pendants
and beads resemble a set found at Desborough, Northants;
the central boss to which the chained pins are attached is
in technique so akin to late Kentish work that it can hardly
be dated before the close of the sixth century. Wiltshire and
the parts immediately adjoining have always been fortunate
in the men who have undertaken the task of elucidating
their antiquities, and have witnessed as much archaeological
excavation as any district of equal size elsewhere in England.
Consequently it is hard to believe that, had they existed,
more relics of Early Saxon settlements would not have been
found. What then are the inferences which the archaeological
evidence suggests? They can hardly be other than that the
historical accounts only represent one side of the story, and
that they do no more than record the doings of one section
of the tribe which ultimately constituted the population of
Wessex. They are those, in short, of a band of invaders
under the leadership of chieftains from whom sprang the
royal house, and nothing is more natural than that their
campaigns should have claimed the chief attention of the
historians. If the traditions are to be credited with even the
minutest particle of truth, nothing is more certain than that
the invaders who entered Britain from the South did not
reach the Thames Valley before the middle of the sixth century,
by which time there are excellent reasons for concluding that

settlements had been established there, dating at least fifty years earlier. It is by a river-route then, and that the Thames, that the bulk of the settlers of Wessex reached the tract of country in which so many cemeteries of this period have come to light. The Saxons have left their traces along the whole line of the Thames Valley almost from its mouth right to its source, and even beyond. The sole objection to this route is the question of London at the time of the invasions, an objection which is based on the position which it appears to have occupied in relation to the Teutonic immigrants. Sir Laurence Gomme, in his work *The Making of London*,[1] comments on the law enacted by Æthelstan to make groups of persons in London responsible for the misdemeanours of any member of the group, in accordance with the Saxon custom prevalent in the surrounding country. From this he concludes that previously the Roman law of individual responsibility had held good. Other traces of Roman law in the City of London have also been observed, particularly that of inheritance. The Roman system of partition as to one third to the wife, one third to the children, and one third as the testator willed, survived down to the reign of George I.

The Chronicle records that the British fled westwards to London after the battle of Creganford, in 456; otherwise it is not mentioned until 604, when Mellitus is supposed to have established the seat of his bishopric there, a good instance of the tendency of the Christian missionaries to connect themselves with places of importance in Roman times. But the idea that London preserved its independence to such an extent as to be able to offer an effective barrier to an invading force moving up the Thames is hardly credible, especially when it is remembered that at a later date when the invasions of the Saxons were ancient history and they in turn had to cope with the attacks of the Danes, London was sacked on no less than two occasions, in the years 841 and 851. Its unpreparedness and its inability to resist attack was the same,

[1] p. 91.

E

whether it were Britons or English who were attacked. Can the results have been different ? Against such an idea can be marshalled the whole results of archaeological research, and they prove conclusively that the Saxon immigrants made full use of the Thames route, unhampered by London or its inhabitants.

To anticipate the description of the cemeteries of Kent, there is an interesting little group of undoubted Saxon origin lying to the west of the Medway, close to the Thames itself, and in many of the cemeteries which lie east of the Medway, and again along the fringe of the northern shore, numerous relics of somewhat similar character have been found. Further westwards another important group comprises amongst others cemeteries at Croydon, Mitcham, and Beddington. In most of them, and in some more than in others, the occurrence of cremation has been observed in the typical hand-made urns of brown ill-fired ware, that are found in large numbers throughout the districts occupied by Anglian and Saxon tribes. So far as the Saxons are concerned, there are strong reasons (see *infra*, p. 57) for believing these cremation burials to be among the early ones ; it is only unfortunate that so seldom is anything found among the ashes which they contain to throw definite light on this point. But along with the skeleton burials [1] were deposited not a few objects which clearly suggest a period not very remote from the beginning of the invasions, as they are such as are commonly associated with the latest graves of the same period in North Germany.

There is therefore a fairly compact group of cemeteries in Surrey which may be regarded as the first considerable area occupied by the Saxons as they advanced up the Thames, and it is not unreasonable to suppose that, if the identification of Wibbandune with Wimbledon is correct, the battle fought there in 565 represents an assertion by the West Saxon rulers of their rights as overlords of this district, in the face of an attempt by the Cantwaras under Æthelbert to extend their power.

---

[1] e. g. at Mitcham, *Proc. Soc. Ant.*, 2 S., xxi. 8, fig. 8 ; and at Croydon, *V. C. H.*, *Surrey*, i. 258, and plate facing p. 257, particularly figs. 7 and 9.

FIG. 8. BUCKLES, ATTACHMENT PLATES, ETC., FROM DORCHESTER, OXON.

Beyond this point, no evidence of settlements of any importance is forthcoming east of Reading. This is easily explained
if it be remembered that south of the Thames between these
two points, and indeed further eastwards also, stretches the
geological formation of the London Clay, and the district
was thus at that date probably densely forested, as was also
the strip lying between the Thames and the Chilterns on the
north bank. The Surrey group is apparently situated on
a thick gravel deposit, or else on the sandy strata of the Upper
Eocene formation. It will be noticed, however, that the few
isolated ·finds occur entirely along the river-bank, and that
none have come to light along the main Roman road running
from London through Staines and Silchester to the west of
England. Silchester, as has been shown, must have fallen on evil
days some time before any settlements were possible.[1] So far as
the Roman roads were concerned, the settlers were essentially
a race with whom traffic by water must, in the absence of
anything but mere tracks in their native country, have been
an everyday occurrence, as the situation of their settlements
there amply demonstrates, and thus, when they first entered
Britain, the habits of centuries were not lightly to be shaken
off, apart from the fact that in keeping to the river, they
ensured an easy retreat in the event of surprise.

Above Reading the centre of the West Saxon settlements is
reached, many of them established long before the band of conquerors working their way up from the south coast could have
reached the district. The archaeological evidence in support of
this contention is very strong and cannot be lightly ignored.
It is at Dorchester, Oxon., that the two earliest burials of this
period, not only in the West, but perhaps in the whole of
England, have been found. Reference has been made to them in
the paper quoted above,[2] but as they have never been fully
published, it may be permissible to do so here. The principal
objects recovered from the graves are shown in the accompanying figure (fig. 8). The accounts are not as clear as might be
desired, but the circumstances of the find seem to have been

[1] F. Haverfield, in *Cambridge Mediaeval History*, i. 380.
[2] See note at foot of p. 51.

as follows. In the course of levelling down a part of the famous Dykes nearest the village of Dorchester, a grave orientated SSE. by NNW. was uncovered, in which lay a skeleton of a man about six feet in height, with knees apparently flexed, and the head at the south-eastern end ; near one shoulder lay the large buckle, among the ribs the narrow riveted bars, and by the thighs the rings with circular faceted attachment-plates. With this skeleton also was found a large bone perforated disc. With another skeleton of moderate size were associated the smaller buckle, the fibula, and a bronze disc (= part of another brooch). Professor Rolleston, into whose hands the objects and the bones eventually came, speaks in his notes, from which these facts are taken, of the woman, so there was evidently little doubt of the sex. Other objects included the bronze strap-tab, a sliding bronze catch, not figured, and some iron fragments and a knife which are no longer preserved. In a letter to Professor Rolleston, the Rev. W. C. Macfarlane, vicar of Dorchester at the time, speaks of some of the objects having been found ' in the end barrow nearest the Thame stream at the Dyke Hills ', and adds that several pieces of iron were apparently thrown into the river by the labourers. It is clear that the graves were those of a warrior and a woman, the man fully equipped with gear and weapons, and the woman wearing brooches and the like, but the importance of the find is that the objects are without exception Teutonic in character, and belong to a period dating to the early half of the fifth century at the latest.[1] The facetted attachment-plates are also identical with examples found in graves at Croydon and Milton near Sittingbourne. The Dorchester find would therefore seem to strongly corroborate what has been said already as to the penetration of the Upper Thames Valley at a quite early period, even were additional evidence lacking.

There are among other things, however, the scabbard-

[1] The exact dating of these relics is not certain. Parallels are known from the fourth century, and this is the date given by Salin (*Månadsblad*, 1894, p. 23). Sir Arthur Evans has dated them even as early as the third century. The latest possible date is here given.

mounts of a sword found at Brighthampton.[1] On the mouth-
piece is a spiral design executed in a manner constantly
associated with the ' Kerbschnitt' technique, while the chape is
ornamented with conventional lions, such as are often found on
metal-work of the latest Roman period in Germany and elsewhere. The general evidence of the larger cemeteries does
not perhaps point to quite so early a date, but it is far earlier
than a wholesale immigration by way of the south coast will
warrant. Professor Rolleston's paper on the cemetery at Frilford, Berkshire,[2] has often been quoted, and his observations
are undoubtedly of great importance. He claims to have
found no less than five types of burials covering a period
from the end of the Roman occupation to Christian Saxon
times, his conclusions being not only based on relics found
with them, but also on the ethnological evidence of skull
types. The typical Roman grave is much deeper than the
rest, with no more than a few late Roman ' minimi', and iron
coffin-nails at most, other interments being in leaden coffins.
These are followed by Saxon graves, for the most part, as
usual in this district, no more than 2 ft. deep ; from these
typical Saxon relics have been recovered. Others again,
deeper and set round with stones, also contained skeletons
of Saxons accompanied by relics, and these are in Professor
Rolleston's opinion the latest [3] ; while interspersed among the
burials were cremation urns of the usual hand-made class.
The value, however, of the cemetery for archaeological purposes lies not so much in the time during which it may have
continued in use, but in the date at which it began to be
used. It is most uncommon, if not unique in Wessex, to find
Saxon graves lying side by side with those of the earlier
Romano-British inhabitants, and it can only be concluded
that the Saxons must have come into possession of the locality
before superficial traces of the cemetery had disappeared.

Judging from the distribution of cremation in Wessex, apart
from considerations connected with the origins of the Saxons

[1] *Archaeologia*, xxxviii. 96, Pl. II.   [2] Ibid. xlii. 417.
[3] This opinion is hardly borne out by the relics themselves.

as a whole, there is strong reason for supposing it to be early;
it occurs with greatest frequency at places situated down the
river, Frilford and Long Wittenham representing roughly
the western limit of its diffusion. The number of cremation
burials occurring at Frilford is uncertain, as the excavation
of only a part of the graves was scientifically watched, but at
Long Wittenham there were 46 cremation urns with 188
burials, representing a very fair proportion of the interments.
On the other hand, in the two most important cemeteries
further up the river, namely Brighthampton and Fairford,
this rite is of rare occurrence, so that it may be concluded
that it was dying out while the Saxons were engaged in
pushing their settlements further westwards.

Apart from such evidence, not much assistance can be
obtained from an examination of associated grave-finds.
The culture is by no means rich, and graves in which
more than one type of characteristic object have been found
are quite uncommon. More useful information is to be
procured from a study of the art-motives used for purposes
of decoration. Though by no means restricted to Wessex,
as the writers of the last century would lead one to suppose, the most distinctive object found there is the saucer
brooch, and somewhat more rarely the 'applied' variety—the
former cast in the solid, the latter made of hammered metal
with the decoration embossed on a separate plate soldered to
the face of the brooch. The patterns employed on these are
of great variety, within the limits referred to in the last
chapter, but amongst them geometric designs predominate.[1]
Of these latter the spiral pattern is the commonest, but stars,
a rhomboidal motive, and others more intricate are also met
with. Their effect is not uncommonly heightened by a
decorative border, the most usual being two typical Roman
designs, the 'egg-and-tongue' and the guilloche. These
borders are also found with zoomorphic designs, but rarely,
and a process of decadence is clearly noticeable in cases where
this combination occurs. Where, then, did the Saxons acquire

[1] For examples see *Archaeologia*, lxiii. 159 ff.

this stock of geometric motives ? The first alternative is that
they brought them with them from their motherland in the
north of Germany. Nevertheless, search made there for
parallels, especially of the use of the Roman borders, proves
unavailing, though a certain number of similar motives occur
in Scandinavia of the fifth century. It is the apparently
extensive survival in England which calls for remark. As
will be shown in a later chapter a difficulty arises here, as the
typical West Saxon brooch is practically unknown in Northern
Europe, but even had it been in process of evolution at the
time of the migration, some parallels to the decoration, however scanty, must have been forthcoming, added to which the
use of any motive having a claim to a Roman origin seems
by the middle of the fifth century to have been almost
entirely ousted by Teutonic zoomorphism. The other
alternative is that these patterns must have been found surviving in some form or other in England, and their continued
employment here well into the sixth century militates most
forcibly against the argument that the Saxons utterly exterminated the natives.[1] Such a design, for example, as that in
figure 9 is impossible from contemporary North Germany,
where such Roman motives as do occur are of the simplest
character. For the invaders to have acquired a knowledge of
these motives, it is absolutely necessary that they must have
been settled in England long before the art to which the
designs belonged had had time to lose its distinctive
character. If the withdrawal of the Legions in 410 resulted in
the rapid disorganization of the country under the constant
inroad of Picts, Scots, and Teutons, it is not likely that art
could have remained unaffected by the general conditions.
Professor Haverfield has even insisted on the definite signs of
a Celtic revival,[2] but Celtic art would have scorned to preserve
many of the purely Roman motives, for example that most
distinctive classical design, the egg-and-tongue border.

[1] The same observation has been made with regard to the attitude of
the Alemanni, Franks, and other Teutonic tribes towards the inhabitants
of the territory within the Roman *limes* (see p. 129).

[2] *The Romanization of Roman Britain*, chap. viii. 62 ff.

The inference is therefore that even putting aside the few examples of the occurrence of objects of early fifth-century manufacture, there must have been not inconsiderable settlements of Saxons in the upper Thames-valley by the beginning of the sixth century at latest. This, however, almost involves a complete reconstruction of the subsequent history of the district as it is given by the early writers. Two events are recorded, firstly a battle at Bedcanford in 571, followed, or as is more reasonable to suppose, preceded by the capture of four towns, the names

FIG. 9. APPLIED BROOCH, FAIRFORD (BRITISH MUSEUM). ¼.
(From *Archaeologia*, lxiii, p. 164.)

of three of which are clearly identifiable with Benson and Eynsham on the left bank of the Thames, and Aylesbury in Buckinghamshire, while the fourth is most probably Luton ; and secondly, a battle in 577 at Deorham (? Dyrham in Gloucestershire) which led to the taking of Bath, Cirencester, and Gloucester. The former suggests that for some length of time the Thames constituted the frontier between the Saxons and the British, and that at Long Wittenham and Benson the two races sat constantly watching one another across the river for half a century or more. In view of the rapid movements of the Saxons indicated in the accounts of the campaigns of 571 and 577 elsewhere, the idea is little short of absurd, and the case of Eynsham is not much better, as the settlement at Brighthampton is on the left bank of the Thames and only about six miles away, and this settlement, judged from the archaeological standpoint, is but little later in date than those at Long Wittenham or even at Frilford. The question of Bedford must be deferred to the next chapter, but it may be said at once that the settlement at Kempston, on the south bank of the Ouse and just opposite Bedford, must have been established a long time before 571. There remain Aylesbury and the other town in the same neighbourhood, whether it be Luton or Lenbury. For these the archaeological evidence fits in better, as the small group of cemeteries near the head-waters of the Thame, such as Bishopstone and Kingston, has yielded no relics which call for such early dating as those from farther west. Indeed, for the most part, the decorated objects show an advanced stage of decadence. From here, indeed, come several of the enormous saucer brooches, none of which must be placed earlier than the last years of the sixth century, as many of them exhibit features which can only be due to influence from Kent.[1] A late penetration of this thickly wooded district is more than probable, but in any case the whole account of the campaign must be regarded with the gravest suspicion. Nor is it otherwise with the date of the capture of Cirencester, whatever may be the truth in regard to the rest of the campaign of 577. At different points along the Thames valley on the north bank of the river from Brighthampton westwards, cemeteries have come to light in many of which the Roman patterns again make their appearance, notably at Broughton Poggs and at Fairford, the latter but eight miles from Cirencester itself. This is one of the largest cemeteries yet discovered in Wessex, and it is impossible to imagine that its graves cover a period much shorter—and this hypothesis is essential if the historical account is accepted without comment—than that, for instance, at Long Wittenham. The cemetery has produced far too many objects belonging to the

[1] *Archaeologia*, lxiii, Pl. XXVIII.

early stages of Anglo-Saxon art, to admit of its being assigned
to a period which began later than the middle of the sixth
century. It has to be remembered that the comparative
youthfulness of the persons buried in Anglo-Saxon graves has
been repeatedly commented on by more than one observer of
the skeletal remains ; it is quite rare to find an old person in
such a grave, and it was recently noted at East Shefford in
Berkshire, that the skeletons of aged women belonged to a different type to those found in the majority of interments. To
suppose that the objects buried along with the deceased were
heirlooms is entirely contrary to all the results of comparative
archaeology both here and on the Continent. Objects found
in association in West Saxon graves are too nearly contem-
poraneous for that ; they cannot, except in rare cases, have
been other than the personal possessions of the deceased in
the first instance.

   The last event in the part of West Saxon history which
is involved in this inquiry is the battle of Fethanleag in 584.
Its identification with Faddiley in Cheshire is a purely
etymological conjecture with nothing else to support it.
Both Chester and Wroxeter must have been sacked by Celtic
attacks long before this date. The latest archaeological evidence from the Roman side connected with Chester does not
appear to extend beyond the end of the fourth century, and
though the excavations at Wroxeter are only in their infancy,
in the first season's work a series of houses has been uncovered
containing no signs of having been occupied after the very
beginning of the fifth century. There was nothing here for
the Saxons to plunder ; the Picts, Scots, or what not had
already forestalled them. No relics of the early Anglo-Saxon
period have been found further west than Shropshire or further
north along the Severn than Worcestershire. But in the three
counties of Gloucestershire, Worcestershire, and Warwickshire a line of cemeteries exists along the line of the Avon
valley which have yielded objects typically Saxon as compared with the Anglian culture to the north. The suggestion
of Fretherne as the site of the battle in Gloucestershire is

consequently more acceptable, but even better is that which identifies it with a place called Fachaleah, mentioned in a charter of Offa of 781 along with Hamtune, identified with Bishop's Hampton near Stratford.[1] It is called Fachanleage in a charter of 966 and Faccanlea in another of 969, and in the former is connected with Upper Stratford, and in the latter with Tidinctune (Tiddington near Stratford). The author of this suggestion comments on the strong West Saxon character of the speech of the district as evidence of its occupation prior to Penda's conquest in the middle of the seventh century. The archaeological material corroborates this view in a very marked degree, and it may be concluded that the battle represents a campaign as the result of which the Saxons successfully occupied the Avon valley. From a point in the neighbourhood of Warwick a small group of finds of West Saxon character extend into Oxfordshire and down the Cherwell valley until a junction is formed with the large settlements in the Thames valley. But a sharp line has to be drawn between these and those on tributaries of the Nene on the other side of the Northamptonshire watershed. This physical feature undoubtedly constituted the boundary between the West Saxons and their neighbours the so-called Middle Angles.

Between the culture of the West Saxons and the Anglian tribes, as illustrated by the grave-finds, there was evidently much in common. The resemblances suggest races of the same general stock, the differences tribal variation within the limits occupied by that stock. Among the similar features may be reckoned the pottery, such objects as bronze-bound wooden buckets, bronze-handled basins, and several varieties of ornaments. Among the brooches the saucer-type certainly predominates, but not a few are of flat penannular form, usually with lightly engraved designs, plain disc brooches and the small square- and cross-headed type similar to those shown in figure 14. A rarity is the large square-headed brooch, profusely

[1] The Rev. C. S. Taylor, in *Transactions of the Bristol and Gloucestershire Archaeological Society*, 1896–7, p. 271.

ornamented and gilt. Three examples from Brighthampton
and Fairford (fig. 10), decorated on the lobes of the cruciform
foot with grotesque human masks in high relief, recall very
strongly examples recently found at Alfriston, Sussex, and this
seems to further bear out the coincidences, already noticed,
with the Sussex culture, which almost suggest influences
diffused from that quarter. The scarcity of the type, as a
whole, in Wessex further serves to corroborate the absence of
intercourse with the north, where it is richly represented.
The form is for the most part the same, but the general style
and ornamentation of the examples found in the Saxon
districts demand a comparatively early date for their manufacture, certainly long before any communication between
the Anglian and Saxon tribes could have been possible, even
if it had been desired by the two races. Again, the cruciform
brooch, so typical of the Anglian culture, is only represented
by four examples in Wessex, two recently found at East
Shefford, and two at Frilford during Professor Rolleston's
excavations.[1] The latter are typologically the earlier, but
none of them connotes more than that the owners possibly
came from the fringe of the Anglian districts in North
Germany, or that among the settlers were a few of Anglian
stock. The beads are not in any way distinctive, and the
buckles are for the most part plain and unassuming in
appearance. There is, however, a type of shield-boss which
appears to be almost peculiar to the south of England which
might throw some light on the particular part of North
Germany from which the Saxons came; but in its more
distinctive form it is most probably of Jutish origin. Best
represented by the remarkable example from Farthingdown,
Surrey (fig. 11 a), its tall, conical, somewhat unwieldy form has
all the appearance of a local variety. Parallels, not always

---

[1] Now in the possession of Cornell University, U.S.A., to the authorities
of which the author is indebted for the opportunity of examining and
photographing them. A detailed account of the grave in which these
brooches were found appears in the *Register of Cornell University*, 1870–1,
p. 52.

Fig. 10. Square-headed Brooch from Fairford.

quite so exaggerated in form, come from Croydon,[1] Sussex (Alfriston), and Wiltshire.[2] Outside the Saxon area they have been found at Sittingbourne and Rochester, Kent, almost on the path of the immigrants, and at Tissington, Derbyshire, the latter an exception in more northerly England.[3] The usual form of boss (fig. 11 b) is, however, that which is associated with men's graves in every part of England.

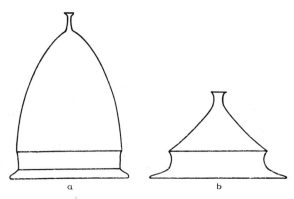

FIG. 11. TYPES OF SHIELD-BOSSES.

The later part of the early period of Saxon history is marked by traces of considerable influence from Kent. Many fine pieces of jewellery, like the two cloison brooches found near Abingdon,[4] and a buckle with garnet setting, are unmistakably of Kentish fabric ; the disposition of the ornament on the later saucer brooches is based on a Kentish model, and many of the finer pieces of glass, for example those found at Cuddesdon[5] and Fairford[6] must have been obtained from Kent, as glass is distinctly uncommon in Saxon cemeteries,

---

[1] V. C. H., Surrey, i. 259.

[2] Catalogue (Devizes Museum), Part I, Stourhead Collection, Nos. 244, 290, 299.

[3] One found at Kempston, Bedfordshire, is in reality from a Saxon district (see p. 81). Other examples come from Ipswich (Archaeologia, lx. 330) and Twickenham, Proc. Soc. Ant., 2 S., xxiv. 329.

[4] Akerman, Remains of Pagan Saxondom, Pl. III.

[5] Ibid., Pl. VI.   [6] Wylie, Fairford Graves, Pl. I.

These importations may not all be of the same date; the glass probably is not; but the rest all belong to the late sixth or early seventh century and thus recall the statement that Æthelbert, baffled in his earlier attempt to extend his influence, had by 597 established a hegemony reaching as far northward as the Humber. The presence of isolated Kentish objects would not amount to much, but the borrowing of designs presupposes conditions of peaceful intercourse, such as would have been impossible in earlier times, if the recorded hostility was an actual fact.

One point has yet to be considered, namely the idea, somewhat prevalent, that East and West orientation entails the supposition that the persons thus buried belonged to a community already coming under the influences of Christian teaching. For statistical evidence only Long Wittenham is of much use. The figures for that cemetery are as follows : out of 188 graves, 54 had the head to the South-West, 96 to the West, 27 towards various points of the compass from North to South, while 11 were uncertain. These figures conceivably represent a fair division of the deceased members ot the community in point of time, allowing for a normal growth of the population, but the baptism of Cynegils at Dorchester as late as 635 does not suggest that the diffusion of the Christian teaching in the surrounding district could have been of very long standing. Typological examination of the grave-finds seems also to show that some of the earlier objects were obtained from graves with a westerly orientation. Paganism must have survived here for some considerable time, with all its accompanying rites and superstitions. The wooden stoup, decorated with bronze plates embossed with biblical scenes and Christian monograms, which was found in a grave with westerly orientation, may conceivably, as has been suggested more than once, be a sign of the infiltration of Christian beliefs among the mass of the population, and the somewhat restricted diffusion of cremation may argue in the same direction, but that the older practices died hard is more than proved by the remarkable discovery at Taplow in 1883.

Here, in a barrow 15 ft. in height and 240 ft. in circumference, situated within the enceinte of the Christian churchyard itself, was found an interment, the body lying with head to the east, and accompanied by a wealth of objects, comprising a gold buckle with cloison settings and filigree ornament, a gold pyramidal stud also set with garnets, the bronze mounts of wooden buckets, and a drinking-horn, a bronze-handled basin with open-work foot, a lobed glass, weapons, among which was an example of the Frankish *angon*, and numerous other objects, pointing to the burial of someone of high rank. The style of the decoration on the bronze mounts and on the goldsmith's work is clearly that of the end of the sixth and beginning of the seventh century ; the gold ornaments, the bronze basin, and the glass must be importations from Kent. Everything, in short, points to a burial with full heathen rites at a date not very distant from the time when the archaeological evidence of burial in the open country comes entirely to an end.

CHAPTER IV

THE ANGLES

ACCORDING to Bede, the tribes which claimed to be of
Anglian stock must have been by far the largest element
amongst the invaders, as he records that from the Angles of
the Danish peninsula were sprung not only the East Angles
and Middle Angles, but also the Mercians, and those settled
north of the Humber, that is within the Anglian kingdom of
Bernicia, and finally 'the other nations of the English'.
What exactly this last vague category is supposed to comprise
would be difficult to say, unless it is intended for the Lindis-
waras. Nor is it quite clear what he intends to convey by the
term Middle Angles, though to judge from later writers it
would seem to imply the inhabitants of the valleys of the
Welland, Nene, and Ouse. Broadly speaking, Bede's statement
is an accurate one, but it would be even unreasonable to
imagine for a moment that Bede, writing in the early eighth
century and engaged on a history of the growth of the
English church, should have troubled to make himself
acquainted with all the facts of the case, even if he had had
the opportunity or the inclination to do so. It is to be
regretted, however, that the venerable priest did not think
well to give in full even the traditions which must have
centred round the Northumbrian kingdom in which he himself lived. As the case stands, however, absolutely nothing
whatever is known of the history of the Anglian tribes
until the year 527, when according to Matthew of West-
minster, not a reliable source of information for this period,
many petty chiefs are said to have arrived in East Anglia
and Mercia, and no specific mention is made of any individual
person until 547, the date given for the landing of Ida in

Northumbria. From this it might be inferred that the first Anglian settlements were for the most part considerably later than the corresponding occupation of districts in the south of England. The problems, then, with which archaeology has to concern itself in the districts apportioned to the Angles are—(i) Is there any evidence which warrants the supposition of settlements of an earlier date, and if so, where were they? and, (ii) Is there anything which suggests the presence, even though only temporary, of other tribal elements which in Bede's day had conceivably been forgotten? What must be the answer to them the subsequent pages of this chapter will try to show.

The distribution of the settlements is in the Anglian districts in many ways exceedingly interesting, as it not only covers country of the most varied character, but also presents some curious contradictions for which it is difficult to furnish an explanation. To take East Anglia first, it will be noticed that while in Norfolk the cemeteries seem to be dotted about in every direction, in Suffolk they are nearly all confined to the valley of the Lark near Icklingham, and the vicinity of Ipswich. But a comparison with the Drift maps (sheets 12 and 16) recently published by the Geological Survey shows that the Norfolk settlements are conditioned by the presence of a wide strip of boulder clay covering the centre of the county. Within this strip, however, occur here and there patches of gravel situated in the valleys of the streams and rivers which intersect the country, and it is close to these patches of open ground within an otherwise thickly wooded area, that the Angles chose to establish themselves, nearly always, as elsewhere, following up the line of a stream until they found a spot to their liking. And in Suffolk the case is precisely the same, though the distribution of the settlements is more local in its character. It is particularly interesting to contrast this fact with the widespread diffusion of places bearing names Anglo-Saxon in origin, as it demonstrates how soon the inhabitants must have ceased to be influenced by this former selectiveness. To the West lay the great inland gulf, as yet undrained, of the Lincolnshire and Cambridgeshire Fens, which precluded all idea of settlement until the rivers emptying into the Wash had been followed for some considerable distance. In Cambridgeshire the cemeteries thus occur near the head-waters of the Cam itself; along the Ouse the cold land affected by the underlying Oxford Clay seems to have offered no attractions; not until the drier soils between Sandy and Bletchley are reached, do the cemeteries make their appearance; in Northamptonshire it is the Great Oolite rocks on the left bank of the Nene that were selected by the settlers, and more particularly, as Mr. Reginald Smith has pointed out,[1] such spots as lay at the junction of the Northampton Sands and the clay of the Upper Lias. On the Gyrwas, who seem to have been closely connected with the Fens, not much light can be thrown, unless a cemetery at Woodstone, Hunts., and the group of finds round Sleaford, including the very large cemetery of nearly 250 graves at Sleaford itself, represent the burials of members of that tribe. Otherwise the finds in Lincolnshire are not very numerous, but they seem to point to settlements established by way of the Ermine street, from a point on the Humber opposite Brough to Lincoln, though as usual some distance from the road.

In the part of Yorkshire which was comprised within the kingdom of Deira a similar state of things is encountered. Settlements along the rivers are vouched for by cemeteries in the valleys of the Aire and near York itself, but the Angles seeking for a congenial soil apparently found themselves barred by the opposition of the British from spreading westwards beyond the Ouse, and therefore made their way into the Wolds of the East Riding. Here, close to numerous barrows of the Bronze Age inhabitants and often in the barrows themselves, the majority of the Yorkshire burials have been found. It is interesting to note how, whenever the invaders penetrated the barrow-areas of England, they made use of the barrows for the interment of their own

---

[1] *V. C. H., Northants,* i. 226.

dead. This practice is not indeed so strongly marked in the South of England, where in Wiltshire Colt-Hoare and others have met with only a few instances. Among the Angles, however, it occurs with great frequency. Not only in Yorkshire but also on the other great barrow-area of the Derbyshire moors secondary interments in Bronze Age barrows are very common, but the use of them as general graveyards, as in the remarkable instance at Driffield,[1] seems to be confined to Yorkshire. In Yorkshire and to the north there is not the same marked avoidance of the Roman roads as elsewhere in the Anglo-Saxon districts; a line of burials north of Brough lie along the road to York, as also others in the valley of Swale in the neighbourhood of the Roman Cataractonium (Catterick), and again at Darlington. Perhaps the most inexplicable point in early Anglo-Saxon archaeology is the astounding lack of evidence for the early settlements north of the Tees, which seem to be demanded by the important part played by Bernicia from the first. Except for the cemetery at Darlington above mentioned, which presumably belongs to Bernicia, finds of any sort of the period are extraordinarily scarce. There would certainly seem to be little warrant for the idea that the Bernician Angles settled the whole district between the Forth and the Tees. A pair of cruciform brooches of Anglian type found with some beads at Corstorpitum[2] was not associated with an interment, and thus conveys no more than the suggestion of settlements in the neighbourhood. The brooches are, certainly, of early sixth-century fabric at latest, while some gold sword-mounts in the British Museum may possibly be no earlier than the seventh-century. Consequently the gap is still to fill. There is one Anglo-Saxon urn in the Royal Scottish Museum at Edinburgh said to come from Aberdeen, but the provenance is very dubious. The idea of an effective occupation of any part of Scotland in early Anglo-Saxon times must be at once jettisoned.

[1] Mortimer, *Forty Years in British and Saxon Burial Mounds of East Yorkshire*, p. 276. [2] *Arch. Aeliana.*, 3 S., v. 406.

The author of the *Historia Brittonum* is responsible for several statements which seriously conflict with the archaeological evidence. First and foremost must be reckoned that which states that Ælla's ancestor in the fifth generation first separated Deira from Bernicia. Ælla's date is 560 to 588, so that, as Professor Oman has pointed out, five generations would carry back the history of the Anglian settlements to the early years of the fifth century. Secondly, there may be noted the statement that Ochta and Ebissa were granted land near the border of the Picts, and thirdly, the voyage of the same two chieftains round Scotland during which they are said to have taken possession of many regions. Professor Oman has concluded from the first two statements, and also from deductions based on the ancestry of Ida, that 'a full century must have elapsed between the first establishment of Anglian settlements on the coast between the Forth and the Humber and the establishment of the " Kingdoms " of Bernicia and Deira'. Considering that elsewhere in England the archaeological evidence of settlements begins quite soon after the first records of the historians, it is incredible that similar evidence should be lacking for Bernicia. It is difficult to understand how the capture of the fortress of Dinguardi (or Bamborough), *c.* A.D. 550, should have been left for Ida to accomplish, if there had been settlements along this coast for a century previous. It is far more probable that the real conquest of Bernicia begins about this date, and that the Darlington cemetery represents the first successful attempt to plant a permanent settlement. A further advance was rendered hazardous by the continual pressure of the native tribes of Clydesdale, the state of Reged, and Galloway. Down to the time when Æthelfrith again combined the two northern kingdoms, the Angles seem to have been in constant conflict with the Britons, the exploits of whose rulers form the subject-matter of the Welsh bardic poems. At Lindisfarne, about the year 572, the Angles even suffered defeat at the hands of the Britons. It is not likely therefore that prior to the battle of Degsastan in 603 there could have been any real security for settlements north of the Tyne at least, and it was not long afterwards that Christianity made its way into Northumbria, and Æthelfrith's successor Edwin became the first Christian ruler of the northern branches of the Angles. Bernicia seems to have stood during the sixth century in the same relation to Deira, as the north of England to the south in Roman times.[1] The former in both cases were held by force of arms; only the latter show anything in the way of peaceable occupation.

The early kingdom of Mercia seems to have included all the territory watered by the Trent. The marshy land on its lower reaches was uninhabitable, and as in the Fens the Angles penetrated right into the interior of the country before they finally found a resting-place. From a point above Brough, Nottinghamshire, the site of the Roman station of Crocolana, the cemeteries become comparatively numerous, extending along the banks of the Trent as far as its junction with the Tame and also close to Tamworth and Lichfield, the seats of the royal Mercian house and the first bishopric of the district. Others occur up the Derwent and, as already mentioned, a large number of burials have been uncovered in the barrows of the Derbyshire moors, the district in short of the Pecsaetan. Southwards the valleys of the Soar and its tributaries were evidently much favoured by the first settlers, as Leicestershire for its size is rich in cemeteries of the period. Doubtless some of the Warwickshire cemeteries also should more properly be reckoned to Mercia, but reasons were given in the last chapter for assigning the lower-Avon group at least to West Saxon extension, prior to the time when the Mercians under Penda became all powerful in this district.

The culture of these Anglian districts, while displaying a close similarity in many respects, yet shows certain divergences which may in some measure be regarded as local. To deal first with the resemblances, it will be found that one and all of the various districts are marked by the appearance of distinctive types of objects, which, though indeed not abso-

---

[1] F. J. Haverfield, *The Romanization of Roman Britain*, p. 20.

lutely unknown are rare outside the Anglian area, and call
for special explanation.   It has often been stated that the
Angles practised cremation, and the statement is perfectly
true, but it is likely to breed a misconception, as it smacks of
the formulation of one of those general rules which are
hardly ever capable of universal application.   It would be
more correct to say that cremation is commoner in Anglian
districts than elsewhere, but that it exists side by side with
burial by inhumation, which is if anything the more usual
rite.   The two rites are found side by side in the same
cemeteries as in Wessex ; on the other hand, large cemeteries
occur in which the one rite predominates, and there is nothing
even here to warrant the one or the other being regarded as
the earlier.   In two instances, the one at Girton near Cambridge and the other at Marton, Warwickshire, cremation
urns contained among other objects what must be regarded
as late examples of saucer brooches ; the Girton brooch is
decorated with the latest type of zoomorphic ornament, the
Marton brooch shows the influence of Kentish models.   As
these two brooches must both belong to the seventh century,
cremation evidently continued to thrive practically down to
to the time when burial in the open country entirely ceased.

In the matter of inhumation burials, there are also some
curious points which are worthy of remark.   The system of
orientation is very irregular ; at Little Wilbraham, Cambridgeshire, the figures were (in each case the position of
the head is indicated)—11 North, 9 North-east, 10 East,
16 South-east, 53 South, 37 West, and 8 North-west.[1]
At Garton Slack, Yorkshire, the 61 burials lay in two
groups, with an interval of about 46 ft. between them ; in
one group the bodies lay with head to the North-west, in the
other to the West.[2]   Mortimer observed that only with
burials in the first group were any relics found and they not

---

[1] Hon. R. Neville, *Saxon Obsequies*, p. 9.   In two cases of the West to
East position, graves 87 and 173-4, the relics were amongst the earliest
from this cemetery.
[2] Mortimer, op. cit., 249.

very numerous; he therefore concluded that they may have belonged to the transition period when paganism and Christianity existed side by side. Another Yorkshire cemetery with easterly orientation was found three miles to the north of that at Garton Slack, again with no relics.[1] At Driffield, on the other hand, in the barrow to which attention has already been drawn, the secondary interments were deposited all round the barrow with head towards the centre, and in another barrow in the same district a similar irregularity of orientation was observed. In both the latter cases characteristic relics were associated with many of the interments. There certainly seems to be a slight justification here for the contention that easterly orientation may be taken as a sign of the march of Christianity. At Sleaford,[2] Lincolnshire, a West to East position was practically universal. Only 12 graves were differently orientated, and in them the bodies lay on their left sides, thus facing north, and with the limbs drawn up in a crouching posture. This latter feature is most unusual as a general practice in a large cemetery containing Anglo-Saxon burials, but it is known elsewhere in Anglian districts, as in the large group of secondary interments in a barrow on Painsthorpe Wold.[3]

As in other parts of Anglo-Saxon England the chief material for comparative archaeological study comes from the graves of women, and it is not always the most striking objects that merit the most attention. Elsewhere the author has already drawn attention to the presence in women's graves in the Anglian districts of bronze clasps, used apparently to fasten the sleeves of the dress (fig. 12 *a*, *c*, *e*, and *f*).[4] Their presence may always be taken as a sign of an Anglian grave or of those of persons living in close contact with an Anglian culture. They occur with greatest frequency in East Anglia, Yorkshire, and what may be termed for convenience the Middle Anglian district; westwards, in the Mercian terri-

---

[1] Mortimer, op. cit., 264. [2] *Archaeologia*, l. 387.
[3] Rolleston and Greenwell, *British Barrows*, p. 135.
[4] *Archaeologia*, lxiii. 186.

tories, they are not so common.   Typically Anglian also are
the chatelaine ornaments, the so-called girdle-hangers, T-
shaped objects of bronze often found in pairs ; whether they
served a useful purpose or were purely ornamental is uncertain
(fig. 12 *d* and *h*).   Among the brooches several varieties are
met with which call for remark ; first and foremost being the
Anglian brooch *par excellence*,[1] the cruciform type.   It is
met with in almost every stage of development, and a ten-
tative scheme of chronology has been evolved by Schetelig
based on a comparative study of analogous forms in
Scandinavia, particularly West Norway.[2]   In his final conclusions he states that the last stages of development, which
this type of brooch underwent before it died out altogether,
belong to the first half of the sixth century, and that, if anything, the margin of difference is in favour of a still earlier date.
For these and other reasons to be considered in subsequent
chapters, the hypothesis that the earliest forms found in
England are not later than about the year 500 seems fully
warranted, especially as in advanced English examples Schetelig
holds that the influence of Scandinavian forms makes itself felt.
It is an interesting commentary, perhaps, on the question of
orientation as a possible test of date, that some of the simplest
cruciform brooches found at Little Wilbraham were found

---

[1] A somewhat serious error has recently been made in regard to these
brooches in the article on ' Englisches Siedelungswesen ', in Hoops' *Reallexikon für germanische Altertumskunde*.   The author in § 14, paragraph 4
(page 601), makes the following statement : ' Archäologische Funde haben
keinen Gegensatz zwischen dem anglischen Norden und dem sächsischen
Süden dargetan, seit die Entdeckungen die Behauptung, dass in vorchrist-
lichen Zeiten die Verbrennung der Toten von den Angeln und die Bestat-
tung von den Sachsen geübt wurde, als falsch erwiesen haben und ebenso
die Theorie zerstörten, dass kreuzförmige Spangen als anglisch und
cupelliförmige als sächsisch anzusehen seien.'   Whatever may be said of
the first and last, the statement in regard to the cruciform brooches is
most misleading.   As shown above, p. 64, and also below, p. 114, they are
very scarce in Southern England and belong to the infant stages of the
type.   The same scarcity and the same infancy is also observable in the
Continental Saxon districts.   In England they are as typically Anglian as
they are Scandinavian on the Continent.
[2] H. Schetelig, *Cruciform Brooches of Norway.*

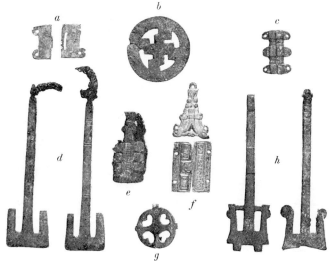

FIG. 12.   BROOCHES, WRIST-CLASPS, ETC., FROM ANGLIAN GRAVES.

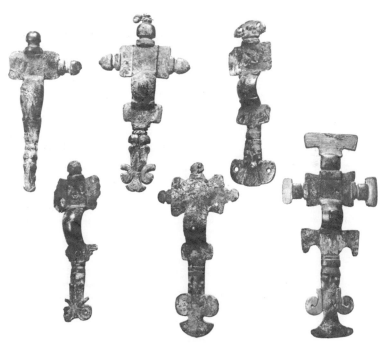

FIG. 13.   ANGLIAN CRUCIFORM BROOCHES.

with skeletons lying with their head to the West.[1] A selection
of specimens of these brooches from East Anglia and Yorkshire is shown in fig. 13. The principal characteristics of
the later forms is increase of size and a predilection for
extravagant decoration, which found an outlet in additions to
the knobs and foot, and particularly in the expansion of the
snout of the animal-head which forms the finial of the brooch,
until it reaches a point at which the original simple head
seems to have been entirely forgotten. Dating, in the purely
Anglian districts, is difficult at any time, but the fact that
the most extravagant forms of this brooch are apparently
unknown north of the Humber is perhaps not without
significance in view of the tradition of the somewhat earlier
conversion of the Northumbrians, as Bede calls them, as
compared with the inhabitants of East Anglia. Much still
remains to be done in the way of close examination of
associated finds in which varieties of this brooch occur ; they
are fairly numerous and might yield some valuable results, not
only for a comparative chronology of this type alone, but also
of other varieties. Another very prevalent type of brooch in
Anglian graves is of annular form ; sometimes it is made of a
narrow ring of bronze, in section rounded above and flat below,
or oval in section, sometimes of a wide flat band of thin metal,
not unlike those found in Sussex. In the large Anglian
cemetery at Sleaford they were especially numerous ; no less
than seventy-three specimens were recovered ; and the narrow
type also figures conspicuously in Yorkshire graves. It would
seem to have been in particular favour in these two districts.
An interesting variety, essentially Anglian, is formed of a disc
of bronze cut à jour sometimes forming a central swastika
motive within a wide border (fig. 12 b and g). In the more
southerly counties of this area, such as Cambridgeshire and
Northamptonshire, among the less imposing brooches one class,
found also in other tribal areas, is richly represented (fig. 14) ;
it is in essence a long brooch but the head displays a wide
variety of shapes ; it may be rectangular, of Maltese-cross

[1] Neville, op. cit., graves 143 and 173, 174.

form, or trilobed, all with numerous fantastic variations; the same ingenuity has been also devoted to the fashioning of the foot. Though also well known elsewhere in England, the large ornate square-headed brooch, usually gilded, occurs in the Anglian area with some frequency. It has occasionally been dubbed Mercian, but there is certainly no reason to regard it as specially such. The numerous specimens found at Ipswich,[1] as also in other Suffolk cemeteries, and in Norfolk and Cambridgeshire, clearly show that no such distinction ought to be made. It is, as a matter of fact, common to all the invading peoples in one form or another, for, though it is scarce in Wessex and Sussex, it is not uncommon in Jutish cemeteries. The reasons will become more apparent after the question of the origin of the invaders has been considered. The decoration of the Anglian examples, though mainly zoomorphic, is occasionally geometric in character, and as this latter decoration is accompanied by greater simplicity of form, examples thus ornamented must rank among the earlier specimens.

Thus far it will be seen that the Anglian culture is fairly uniform in character, and that, apart from small local divergences and predilections, there is little to admit of the Anglian area being split up into divisions which might be in any way regarded as synonymous with a different Continental origin. In a group of counties, however, comprising Cambridgeshire, Bedfordshire, Northamptonshire, and Rutland, the occurrence of certain types undoubtedly demands further explanation. The first is the saucer brooch and the 'applied' variety. Its diffusion in Anglo-Saxon cemeteries has been dealt with elsewhere [2] at considerable length. A general idea of their distribution can be obtained from the map (fig. 15); further than this it is only necessary here to state the main facts and the inferences which may be drawn from them. This class of brooch has often been described as West Saxon, and where the occurrence of any examples in places which apparently

[1] *Archaeologia*, lx, part 2, 333, figs. 7 and 9.
[2] Ibid., lxiii. 159 ff.

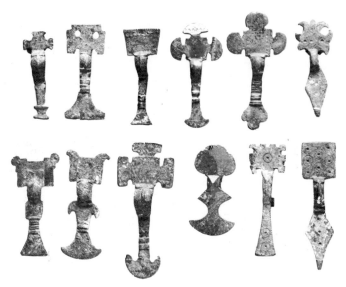

FIG. 14. SMALL BRONZE BROOCHES OF VARIOUS TYPES,
CHIEFLY FROM CAMBRIDGESHIRE.

lay in districts outside the limits of early Wessex has been noted, the brooches themselves have usually been labelled West Saxon. There appears, however, to be very little justification for doing so. Without contending that the line of any watershed formed a real obstruction to expansion, the definite manner in which the Anglo-Saxon burying-places, when marked out on a map, show themselves in groups along the course of rivers, suggests that the Teutonic method of settlement contributed in a large measure towards fixing the tribal boundaries. One such boundary was the watershed separating the rivers which disembogue into the Wash from the Thames, the Warwickshire Avon, and their tributaries. Eastwards of this line the type of brooch in question is almost as prevalent as on the western side, particularly in the counties of Northampton, Bedford, and Cambridge (fig. 15),[1] but with the difference that the 'applied' form and zoomorphic ornament are immensely predominant. These two phenomena by themselves would be of little value as arguments for a division into geographical groups, but, if any value at all is to be attached to the historical accounts of West Saxon expansion, it is certain that they could not have reached the Ouse Valley until quite late in the sixth century, after the date given for the battle at Bedcanford in 571. Neither peaceful trade nor tribal movements through the district between the Thames and the Ouse could have been possible sooner, and as a matter of fact the area east of the watershed has produced equally good examples of early designs on this class of brooch, showing clearly that the inhabitants must have been acquainted with it long before their western borders put an end to West Saxon expansion in an easterly direction. Nor can it be a mere coincidence that one design which is particularly prevalent in this easterly area of diffusion is found on the Ouse at Kempston near Bedford, and at various cemeteries in Cambridgeshire, where also most of the early examples occur. Another interesting point is that this type is found in greater numbers in some

---

[1] *Archaeologia*, lxiii. 163, fig. 4.

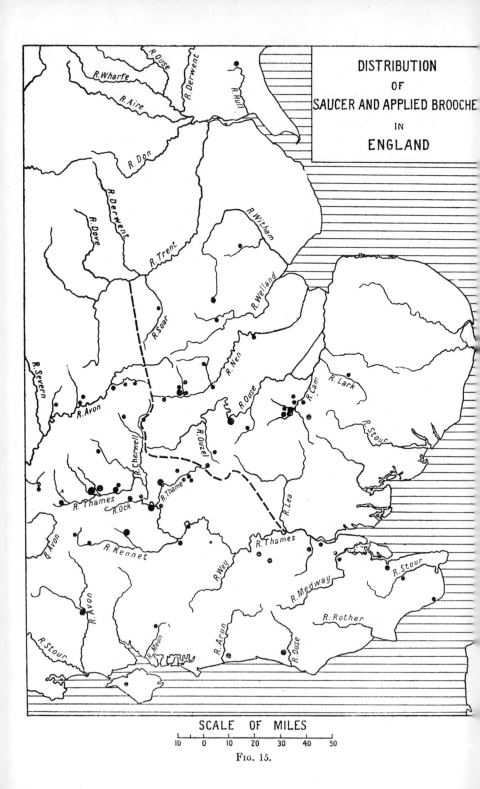

DISTRIBUTION
OF
SAUCER AND APPLIED BROOCHE
IN
ENGLAND

SCALE OF MILES

10 0 10 20 30 40 50

FIG. 15.

cemeteries than others, the most richly endowed in this respect being Barrington, Haslingfield, and Linton in Cambridgeshire, Duston near Northampton, and Kempston. Only part of the Barrington cemetery was scientifically excavated, but both here and in a minor degree at Linton and Haslingfield typical Anglian relics have been found, while at Duston and Kempston they are scarce or entirely wanting, particularly the typical cruciform brooch, though this is well known from Northamptonshire. It has already been shown that the saucer brooch is typical of the Saxon districts of Sussex and Wessex, and it is not unknown even in Essex.[1] It is curious therefore to find this Saxon trait in the culture of the district which is generally assigned to Bede's Middle Angles. A possible explanation seems to lie in the assumption that at one time, and this the earliest, a Saxon tribe had been in sole possession. Alongside of the cemeteries in Cambridgeshire where the type of brooch occurs, other large ones, like those at Little Wilbraham and Girton, have been found containing Anglian types pure and simple, with the exception in each case of one specimen of the Saxon brooch, both, however, with comparatively late decoration. It looks, therefore, as if some subsequent invasion by a tribe or tribes of Anglian stock had dispossessed the earlier settlers in Cambridgeshire, and that the cemeteries further west, where the Saxon brooch occurs most freely, are those of parts of the tribe retreating before the new immigrants. It is equally possible, however, that the settlement of the district by immigrants of different stocks was a peaceful one, but that the Angles by force of their numerical superiority gradually absorbed the Saxon element, so that by Bede's time the fact that Saxons had ever existed at all in the district had been entirely forgotten. The process, however, was sufficiently slow not to eliminate certain aspects of the Saxon material culture before the close of the pagan period.

As in the territory occupied by the Saxon tribes, so in the

---

[1] A pair found at Feering in that county (*Essex Naturalist*, ii. 124) has been brought to the author's notice since the publication in *Archaeologia* of the paper already referred to.

Anglian districts, here and there traces occur of relations of some kind with Kent.   Such evidence as is capable of analysis suggests that this intercourse did not become active before the latter part of the sixth century.   Here again, therefore, the powerful influence exerted by Æthelbert outside Kent is doubtless responsible for any objects of Kentish workmanship found in such Anglian cemeteries as Ipswich, Little Wilbraham, and Girton.   It is somewhat strange that more Kentish objects have not been found in the Anglian territory, considering how much richer and finer is the workmanship displayed on the products of the Kentish workshops.   It only serves to show how superficial was the intercourse between the different tribes in the early stages of their history.   The hegemony of Æthelbert as far north as the Humber was due evidently to his personality alone.   With his death it ceased, and likewise the clear signs of influence from Kentish culture at the end of the sixth century seem to vanish.

CHAPTER V

The Origin of the Angles and Saxons

BEFORE entering on a discussion of the archaeological aspects of this question, it may be well to give a brief summary of the conclusions which have been arrived at along other lines of research. Chief among these are probably those which have been yielded by a comparison of the Anglo-Saxon language and its various dialects with the remains of the old north Germanic language-group. It is agreed that Anglo-Saxon has close affinities to Low-German ('Platt-Deutsch' or 'Niedersächsisch'), and that its diffusion in early times extended over practically the whole of North Germany and parts of Holland.[1] The limit northwards of this group is a line drawn across the Danish peninsula practically coterminous with the present political division between Denmark and Germany. At this point it impinges on a Scandinavian group of dialects. At this northern end of the Low-Saxon area of diffusion, and also in the north-west angle of Holland, appear intrusive elements known as Frisian, which are closely akin to the Kentish dialect. Excluding these, therefore, it would seem that the other English dialects might have come from almost any part of North Germany, but the area is further limited by the known extension of Slav tribes almost up to the Elbe at the time when the migrations to England were in full swing. Difficulties have arisen from the presence of a large number of words in Anglo-Saxon which point to close intercourse with races living within the limits of the ancient Roman Provinces, and these have led some philologists to argue a temporary sojourn of certain elements among the Anglo-Saxon settlers in the vicinity of the Rhine. To support this hypothesis, the promoters of the theory have had to fall

[1] O. Behagel, *Geschichte der deutschen Sprache*, in Paul's *Grundriss*.

back, partly on a few obscure passages in ancient writers which seem to connote the presence of Saxons and possibly even of Angles near the mouth of the Rhine, and partly on the known existence of a Saxon shore along the northern coast of Gaul, which for the purpose of this theory has sometimes been construed to mean a coastal strip in which the Saxon pirates established themselves either by force or by permission grudgingly given, but born of a very impotence to do otherwise. The merits of this theory lie in the avoidance of all necessity of denying the veracity of Bede, whose writings have been taken as a working basis for research of every kind into the problems of the origin of the Anglo-Saxon race. According to Bede, all the Saxon tribes came from the region ' now called Old Saxony '. Northwards of them was Anglia, the motherland of the English Anglian settlers, and this country lay between the Continental provinces of the Saxons and Jutes, so that the latter in Bede's estimation must have come from the Danish peninsula. The exact extent of the region which he designates by the name Old Saxony is uncertain, but Professor Chadwick regards it as comprising an area stretching from the Yssel to the Elbe in an easterly direction, and southwards to a line somewhere in the vicinity of the Lippe which ran eastwards to the Harz, that is the western half of the region which Behagel assigns to the ' Low-Saxon ' language. In addition to this, western Holstein was also occupied by a tribe who seem to have been Saxons. The situation of Anglia should therefore, according to Bede, be practically that of modern Schleswig, and in consequence his Jutes would fall either in the district in which a Frisian dialect still survives, or still further north in the Danish territory of Jutland.

Some light from another quarter has been thrown on the origin of the settlers by the researches of Meitzen[1] into the various systems of land-tenure existent in Europe. He has demonstrated the existence of entirely different systems in the regions east and west of the Weser. In the latter the

---

[1] *Siedelung-und Agrarwesen der West-und Ostgermanen.*

hamlet or isolated homestead ('Einzelhof') prevails, while from the Weser to the vicinity of Kiel the land was parcelled out into strips round the village which formed the nucleus of the system ('Gewanndorf'). The line of cleavage between the two systems is in North Germany extraordinarily well marked, and though Meitzen is not so successful when he seeks to prove the existence of a similar condition of things in England, yet undoubtedly the same distinction does to some extent hold good. In Kent, Sussex, South Hampshire, and Dorset, he pronounces the hamlet system to be the prevailing type, whereas northwards from these districts the nucleated village can be clearly observed. Meitzen's results consequently are not much at variance with those of historical or philological research, except that they entail a rejection of Bede's homeland of the Jutes, in favour of the alternative preferred by many philologists, who place them in the western Frisian district, or north-western Holland.

In order to fully comprehend the archaeological side of the question, it is necessary to remember first that with the exception of Holland, no part of this north-European region was ever more than temporarily subject to Roman domination. After the attempts of Drusus, Tiberius, and Germanicus to extend the Empire to the Elbe, the land occupied by the northern Germanic tribes never suffered again from invasion by the Legions. There in consequence the north European culture still continued to develop uninterrupted by an interval during which the civilization of Rome reduced everything to the stereotyped sameness which is its predominant characteristic throughout the Western Empire. Trade with the Empire certainly did much to modify the evolution of Teutonic culture as a whole, but its influence was confined to such effects as were produced by the importation of Roman manufactures. That from these the Germans derived a certain number of new ideas is clear from many of the designs and forms which are to be met with on objects of German fabric, but they are unmistakably brought into line with the prevailing German taste of

the time. But towards the end of Rome's career as an impe-
rial power in the West, the Teutonic element in the culture
reasserts itself, and by the end of the fifth century it would
be difficult to find a single object in northern Germany or
Scandinavia which, taken by itself, would ever suggest that
Roman influences had contributed even the smallest quota
towards the development of either its form or its ornamentation. Nothing perhaps demonstrates more clearly how
complete was the process of jettisoning everything Roman than
the Teutonic zoomorphic ornament. It has been described as
'the only really original form of art that was created by the
prehistoric peoples north of the Alps'. This description
denies even the initial suggestions from Roman art motives,
which have been remarked upon in the second chapter. It
only shows how thoroughly any traces of external influence
must have disappeared for such a denial to be possible at all.
Among the causes which largely contributed to this result
were the movements of the Teutonic tribes as early as the third
century. The northern stream of migration, which set in so
strongly in the fourth and fifth centuries, is already heralded
in North Germany and Scandinavia at the end of the third and
beginning of the fourth, by finds of objects similar to those then
in vogue in Southern Russia.[1] The process of elimination of
the Roman element is admirably illustrated by the numerous
moor-finds which are such a feature in the archaeology of this
period. In the earliest of these finds (c. A.D. 250), such as
at Vimose, the constituent objects without exception bear the
impress of Roman influence ; at the next stage, represented by
the famous Thorsbjerg find, the Roman element is per-
ceptibly less, and this find can be dated by coins to about
A.D. 290. By the time that the first Nydam deposit was
made, the Roman element has nearly vanished and the
Teutonic style is everywhere predominant. This find can on
various grounds be assigned to the last half of the fourth
century. The disappearance of everything Roman and the

---

[1] O. Montelius, *Den nordiska jernålderns Kronologi* (5th period),
(*Svenska Forminnesföreningens Tidskrift*, x).

absolute assertion of the Teutonic element comes in the fifth century with such finds as Kragehul and Sjöröd. In view therefore of the date at which the migrations to England began, it is but natural to expect that its origins in North Germany should exhibit the features of the last two groups of moor-finds. But as has been shown, certain factors contributed to keep alive the Roman element for a longer period in England, so that, at the time when it had utterly disappeared in northern Europe, it was still flourishing in certain parts of England.

The conditions under which the relics of the pre-migration period are found in northern Europe are, apart from the moor-finds, exactly comparable with those of Anglo-Saxon England. As in England, no traces whatever remain of any settlements; the material for archaeological study is almost entirely derived from a series of urn-fields extending from Denmark to Holland (fig. 16). A few examples of these urns-fields may serve to give some idea of the conditions under which the deceased were buried and of the relics which accompanied them.

(i) *Borgstedt*.[1] This huge urn-field, situated about half a mile north of Rendsburg in Schleswig, first became known in 1876, and a part of the discoveries are now in the Kiel Museum. It lay partly on the south side of a large mound and partly beyond the base. On the slope itself the urns were buried about $1\frac{1}{2}$ ft. deep, and usually covered with a stone; beyond the mound the depth diminished to about nine inches and a cover was rare. The number of urns actually discovered was reckoned at between 800 and 1,000.[2] One and all contained burnt bones. No information is available for the greater part of the finds, but those in the Kiel Museum allow a fair estimate to be formed of their character. The urns themselves are very varied, both in form and

---

[1] J. Mestorf, *Urnenfriedhöfe in Schleswig-Holstein*, 69.

[2] They stood in some places as much as half a yard apart, but in others they were so tightly packed together that 'there was hardly room to insert a knife-blade between them'.

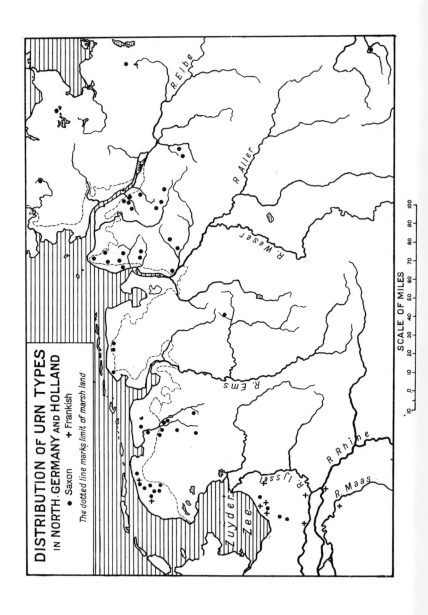

DISTRIBUTION of URN TYPES
IN NORTH-GERMANY AND HOLLAND

● Saxon   + Frankish

The dotted line marks limit of marsh land

SCALE OF MILES

10 0 10 20 30 40 50 60 70 80 90 100

R. Elbe

R. Aller

R. Weser

R. Ems

R. Rhine

R. Maas

R. Ijssel

Zuyder Zee

decoration, but they are precisely comparable with examples from many English grave-fields, more particularly those of the Anglian districts. Judging from their contents, they cover a period which included the fourth century and part of the fifth, and it is noteworthy that among the later relics found in the urns are a few cruciform brooches, all of which represent the earliest stages of the evolution of this type from another which occurs both at Borgstedt and in the Nydam moor-find.[1] Of one other variety (compare fig. 14) which is extremely common in England, a few examples were found at Borgstedt, and this has been noted as the only known occurrence of this type in North Germany.[2] Swords, large spears, and shield-bosses are all wanting ; beads are mostly of plain colours, blue, green, red, and yellow, but fragments of molten glass vouched for the presence of occasional examples of more decorative types.

In Holstein large urn-fields of this class are apparently scarce. Fräulein Mestorf, writing in 1886, cannot cite a single example.[3] The eastern part of the province was eventually occupied by the Slavs, and on the western side lay the marsh-lands of the Ditmarschen district. From the islands of Amrum and Föhr, however, a few finds are known, remarkable chiefly for the difference of the pottery from that found at Borgstedt. Some of it has a fine black burnish, and includes handled vases, which are unknown from the Borgstedt urn-fields.

(ii) *The province of Hanover.* This was clearly one of the most thickly populated districts of North Germany during the period which preceded the migrations to England. It is also the district which is most closely connected by tradition with the Saxons. Thither they are said to have come from farther north, landing at Haduloha (Hadeln, near Cuxhaven), but their exact origin was a matter of dispute. The version which derives them from the Angles or Danes is

---

[1] See especially op. cit., Plate IX, figs. 1, 2, 3, 8–11.
[2] Salin, op. cit., figs. 160–2.
[3] Op. cit., p. viii.

probably not far from the mark, as many of the forms which
are found among the pottery can be traced to others which
are found in urn-fields of the second and third centuries
in Jutland. There was undoubtedly a movement of tribes
southwards in the fourth and fifth centuries, the two outstanding instances being the migrations of the Burgunds and
Langobards from the north to central and southern Europe.
The many points of similarity in the genealogies of the
Saxon and Anglian rulers in England are thus partly corroborated by archaeological evidence. A large number of important cemeteries have been excavated in Hanover; among
them those of Perleberg, Wehden, Rebenstorf, Quelkhorn,
and Westerwanna may be particularly mentioned. All those
of any importance are situated on the edge of moorland
which overhangs the marshy flats along the left bank of the
Elbe and the east bank of the Weser, and its tributary the
Wimme. These cemeteries are without exception urn-fields.
Cremation is the universal method of burial; inhumation
may practically be said to be unknown. A few isolated
instances of this practice have been found both here and in
Schleswig-Holstein, but it is extremely difficult to gauge
their import in relation to the thousands of urns of the same
period. In the province of Hanover, as at Borgstedt, the
urns closely resemble many English examples, though amongst
the extraordinary multiplicity of shapes which this hand-
made ceramic includes, it might be difficult if not impossible
to discover any two exactly alike. At Perleberg [1] they were
buried at a depth ranging from 14 to 48 centimetres, and
usually a little distance apart. Müller records the occurrence
of seven urns within an area of 24 sq. ft. It was noticed
here, as elsewhere in the province, that a gradual development could be traced in the technique and decoration of
the urns; the earlier are generally reddish in colour and
of a simple globose form with short neck and without
decoration, while the later specimens are of an even shade

---

[1] J. H. Müller, *Vor- und frühgeschichtliche Altertümer der Provinz Hannover*, 177.

Fig. 17.   Equal-armed Brooch from Anderlingen, Hanover.

of brown and exhibit the utmost diversity both in form and decoration. As long ago as 1855, Kemble drew attention to the close similarity of the urns from Anglo-Saxon cemeteries to those from Stade and other places in this province, and from the close analogies observable in the character of the relics which they contained, he pronounced them to be probably contemporary.[1] This opinion was based on such objects as tweezers, shears, and the like, all of them types which do not exhibit any marked variety throughout the period of the migrations themselves and that of the resultant settlements. The advance which has been made in recent years in the application of the comparative method in archaeology now renders it possible to arrive at more precise ideas as to the relative dates of these Continental cemeteries and those of Anglo-Saxon England. Among the most useful material for this purpose are various classes of metal objects. Firstly, attention may be drawn to the equal-armed brooches (fig. 17). Of this particular variety of the form, with its semi-classical decoration, several examples are now known from this province, and they do not seem to have been found outside it. This fact is therefore of the highest importance, as it demonstrates beyond a doubt that the few specimens known from English soil must have come from this district. As they are essentially women's gear, it may fairly be presumed that their discovery at Haslingfield and Little Wilbraham in Cambridgeshire, and Kempston, Bedfordshire, denotes the presence of settlers belonging to a tribe which had emigrated from Hanover.[2] That they entered England from the east is made quite clear by the fact that the earlier examples came from Cambridgeshire. The Kempston specimen appears to be a poor copy made in England itself. Further evidence of the same kind exists in support of the hypothesis, advanced in the last chapter, that Middle Anglia was at one time partly settled by a Saxon population. At

---

[1] *Horae Ferales*, 229.

[2] See also *Månadsblad* for 1894, and *Jahrbuch des Provinzial-Museums zu Hannover* (1907-1908), 13 ff.

Girton, Stamford, and Kempston examples of so-called
' window-urns' (*Fensterurnen*) have been found. The title is
derived from a small piece of thick glass which has been in-
serted, usually in the bottom of the vase, while the clay was
still soft. That this glass passed through the process of firing
unharmed, is in itself ample proof of the perfunctory nature
of that operation. Several of these ' window-urns' are known
from Hanover ; a remarkable specimen from Hohenwedel [1]
has an additional ' window' in the side of the vase. Cruciform
brooches, though not very numerous, are by no means unknown,
but they one and all belong to the simpler forms. Probably
no example from this region can be dated later than A.D. 450
This would account for their scarcity in purely Saxon districts in England and would further support the presumptively
Saxon character of the settlements at Duston and Kempston.
Yet another class of objects which can be paralleled from
England is well represented in the cemeteries of Hanover.
Particular attention has already been drawn to the remarkable
find from Dorchester, Oxfordshire. Buckles and belt-fittings
of a similar kind have been found as part of the contents of
cinerary urns in several of these North German cemeteries,
but as they are also known from the earlier Frankish
cemeteries of the period in Belgium, it would be hard to
designate the probable provenance of the English examples,
were it not for the fact that in one instance they were
associated with a brooch such as never occurs in Belgium,
and also that the majority of them have been found in what
were essentially Saxon districts. There are, however, some
distinctive types which appear either only as isolated examples
in North Germany or not at all. One of these is the
characteristically Saxon saucer brooch. Considering how
numerous they are in this country, it is surprising that
more have not come to light on the Continent. Examples
from North European sites are exceedingly scarce and they
include a pair found with a cremation burial at Alten Buls

---

[1] Now in the Provincial Museum at Hanover.

in Hanover [1]; another accompanied a skeleton interment at Harmignies, near Mons, Belgium. These are all of the true saucer type, one with a cruciform spiral, the other with a running spiral design. What may be regarded as an example of the 'applied type' comes from an inhumation burial at Kruft, near Andernach; this also is decorated with running spirals. Such widely scattered examples do not unfortunately throw any very satisfactory light on the origin of the type as a whole. The suggestion that an impetus was given to its development by a small cupelliform variety of the size of a fair-sized button is more than likely, especially in view of the numerous examples found in Sussex. It has also been suggested elsewhere [2] that a North German brooch, which is by no means uncommon in these cremation cemeteries, may also have been partly responsible. But the type whose absence from these cemeteries is even more remarkable is the large square-headed brooch. Indeed, except for the isolated specimens from Borgstedt already mentioned, the smaller variety of the same type is also unknown. One of the commonest brooch-types from these cemeteries is a Teutonic development of the Roman cross-bow type. It is always of small size, but it is interesting on account of its occasional association with objects which are among the rare occurrences in English cemeteries, and also because it is usually decorated with faceting closely akin to that which appears on the earliest cruciform examples. It belongs, in short, to the end of the fourth century. Westwards from the part of Hanover lying between the Elbe and the Weser, a few cemeteries occur along the coast between the Weser and the Ems, but none appears to represent settlements of any great importance.

(iii) In *Holland*, however, another interesting group is to be met with. Here, on the fringe of the moorlands of Gelderland and Drenthe, as also in the low-lying flats of Groningen and Friesland, ample traces of Saxon occupation are to be

[1] *Archaeologia*, lxiii. 194, fig. 22.
[2] Ibid., 193.

found. In the latter district the burials are found in the 'terpen' (or, as they are called in Groningen, 'wierden'), the huge mounds which thrust themselves out from the low-lying lands within the dykes and which mark the site of a village or hamlet. At Hoogebeintum quite a large number of typical Saxon urns containing ashes have come to light, but alongside of these there have also been burials in wooden coffins and in hollowed tree trunks.[1] Both there and at Beetgum the Saxon pottery was accompanied by vases of Frankish type, wheel-made and differently ornamented, one of which at least contained remains of a cremation burial. The Saxon urns may be attributed to the spread of the Saxon tribes westwards in the fourth century, probably about the time when the Roman Emperor Julian gave permission to the Franks then living in Holland to cross the Rhine and settle in modern Brabant. The distribution of Saxon and Frankish urn-types in the Netherlands can be seen on the map (fig. 16) and it is clear that the Rhine was the limit of Saxon expansion. As the Franks did not practise cremation, the Frankish vases containing ashes may be merely instances of Frankish pottery used for this purpose by Saxon invaders. So far as the contents of the Saxon urns are concerned, brooches of simple cruciform type seem to point rather to Schleswig than to the Elbe districts for the origin of the settlers, the more so as quite a large number of these brooches, some far more advanced in point of evolution, have been found in various places in Friesland and Groningen (fig. 18). One possibility that their presence in such numbers in this corner of Europe may have more than a purely archaeological significance will be discussed in the final chapter. One or two, however, are so strongly reminiscent of English examples that it is interesting to recall that Procopius[2] records a fight between Angles from England against Radajis, king of the Warni, living on the coast of Holland, on account of his repudiation of an Anglian princess in favour of Theudebert's

[1] P. C. J. A. Boeles, *De Friesche Terpen*, 21, and figs. 17–22.
[2] *De bello Gothico*, iv. 20.

FIG. 18. CRUCIFORM BROOCHES FROM FRIESLAND.

daughter. The possibility of intercourse with Anglian districts is not therefore entirely excluded as an explanation of these apparently English specimens.

So far then, a comparison of the archaeological remains from North Germany and Holland with those of Anglo-Saxon England emphasizes certain marked points of difference:

(i) The whole culture of the Continental homelands is clearly of earlier date, and not only is this so, but so scarce are the actual links connecting it with that of England, that it is difficult to bring the two into immediate connexion with one another. It may be said that the archaeological material from the German cemeteries breaks off, almost entirely, exactly at the very earliest point at which anything comparable appears in England. It is scarcely conceivable that among the very numerous cemeteries of North Germany so little overlap should be observable, had the invaders of England emigrated direct from this part of the Continent. There seems to be lacking an interval of some kind, probably quite brief, during which the culture of the invaders reached the stage of development which characterizes its first appearance in England. There are some faint indications, philological and historical, that this interval may have been passed in the north of France, but, in spite of the definite record of settlements of Saxons as far south as the Loire, the archaeological traces of Saxon occupation of any part of the tract of coast of Gaul known as the Saxon shore, are almost as non-existent as the evidence of a similar nature for the occupation of the Saxon shore in England. If this implies that, after all, the migrations started direct from North Germany and Holland, then the process of evolution at work in the culture of the invaders must have been unusually rapid, and finally a large number of the settlements must have come into being considerably earlier than any historical documents will warrant.

(ii) In addition, however, to these rapid changes in the material relics of the Anglo-Saxons, a further difficulty arises from the startling divergence in the burial-rites on the two sides of the North Sea. As has been noted, except in Holland and in a few other isolated instances elsewhere, cremation is universal, and yet in this country inhumation is met with at the very beginning of the Anglo-Saxon occupation. So much so, that it might even be used as evidence of direct migration, since, while the equal-armed brooches so distinctive of Hanover have all except one been found with cremation burial, the three examples from English soil all came from inhumation graves. Scarcity of fuel, one of the reasons offered in explanation of burials by inhumation in North Germany, will hardly hold good for Saxon England, even in districts like Kent and Sussex, where the cemeteries are for the most part on the open downs.[1]

The difficulties in the way of equating the archaeological remains of any Saxon district in England with those of any particular part of North Germany are very great. Apart from the few parallels already noticed, it might almost be said to be impossible. And the task becomes no simpler when the origins of other tribal elements among the Anglo-Saxon invaders are subjected to investigation. Bede brings the Angles from a district in the Danish peninsula which he says is called Angulus, evidently the district now known as Angeln, between the Schlei and Flensburg Fiord,[1] and he adds that the emigration to England entirely depopulated the district. From the situation of this district, it is evident that if any special cemeteries are to be assigned to the ancestors of the Angles of England, that at Borgstedt must certainly be one of them. The difference of time between the latest relics from this district and those from England is not so great as in some Saxon districts. The same phenomenon is, however, equally observable here as in other parts of North Germany, namely that the culture ends at the very point at which it begins in England, but there are some features in the English culture which suggest more protracted

---

[1] For Beowulf's pyre wood is spoken of as brought from a distance (*Beowulf*, l. 3110 ff.).

[2] See Chadwick, op. cit., 104.

relations with northern Europe than can be explained by the
wholesale migration suggested by such a cemetery as Borgstedt. They speak, moreover, for connexion with districts
still further north. Schetelig, while admitting that the
earliest cruciform brooches from England are akin to those
of Denmark,[1] claims that in more advanced specimens there
are clear traces of Norwegian influence. In this connexion
Schetelig regards central England as the route by which
many imported objects, such as bronze vessels and glass,
were introduced into Norway, in preference to a direct
Frankish or South English source, to which these imports
were attributed by Rygh.[2] He even considers the ties between England and Norway to have been of some considerable
duration. As further evidence of relations with the western
side of the Scandinavian peninsula, there has been adduced
the occurrence at Addington, Northamptonshire, of a handled
vase of peculiar form, such as is well known from contemporary Norway. A few examples are, however, known from
Denmark and North Germany, so that this unique specimen
from England carries but little weight as evidence.[3] More
important are the sleeve-clasps to which attention was drawn
in the last chapter. These are apparently unknown in
North Germany,[4] but somewhat similar clasps have been
found both in Denmark and Norway, as also another variety,
usually of silver and formed on the hook-and-eye principle,
with spirally coiled terminals to the loops, which is
represented by several examples in the Anglian cemeteries
of this country.[5] But of still greater importance are the
large square-headed brooches. These again, as already noted,

---

[1] *The Cruciform Brooches of Norway*, 102.

[2] *Prähistorische Zeitschrift*, iv. 365.

[3] Sophus Müller, *Ordning af Danmarks Oldsager*, ii, No. 302.

[4] The author has been unable to discover a single specimen in any of
the important museums between Kiel and Emden, beyond what appears
to be a fragment from Westerwanna. (Morgenstern Museum, Geeste-
münde, No. 2439.)

[5] Cf. Müller, op. cit., ii, No. 508, and G. Gustafson, *Norges Oldtid*, 72
and figs. 296, 297.

are unknown from North Germany, but in both Scandinavia and Denmark they form one of the most remarkable features in the antiquities of this period. It is unnecessary to refer to specific examples, as they are illustrated in all the principal works on Scandinavian and Danish archaeology. No mention has been made of the bracteates, many of the English examples of which seem equally to demand a similar provenance, as most of them have been found in Kent; since they have an important bearing on the archaeology of that county, they are left for subsequent discussion. One point in regard to the history of Kent may, however, be forestalled here with advantage, namely the archaeology of Jutland. For, if the origin of Anglian antiquities seems to demand extension as far northwards as Norway, it is hardly probable that the region intervening between that country and the Continental Anglia should not have been also responsible for a part of the 'Anglian' culture. At a somewhat earlier period in Jutland, slightly before that of the Borgstedt cemetery, cremation burials, often in tumuli, are fairly common, while skeleton burials are not so numerous as in other parts of Denmark.[1] During the period, however, which corresponds more exactly to that of the settlement of England, the cremation graves in Jutland are unpretentious and as a rule but poorly furnished with relics.[2] But amongst them a few small cruciform brooches found in graves should be noticed, forming part of thirty examples from Denmark, known prior to 1895, of which the majority come from Jutland. Everything points to a close resemblance of the culture of this province of Denmark to that of Schleswig to the south of it. The greatest stress requires to be laid on this fact, as it has an important bearing on the archaeology of Kent.

---

[1] Sophus Müller, *Nordische Altertumskunde* (*Deutsche Ausgabe von Dr. O. L. Jiriczek*), ii. 117.
[2] Ibid., pp. 191, 192, and *Ordning af Danmarks Oldsager*, ii. 54.

CHAPTER VI

The Jutes

'From the Jutes are descended the people of Kent and of the Isle of Wight, and those also in the province of the West Saxons who are to this day called Jutes, seated opposite to the Isle of Wight.' Thus the venerable Bede; and the archaeologist, here at least, apart from the problem of the name Jutes and their origin, can find little fault with Bede's statement, whatever difficulties may stand in the way of unqualified acceptance of other traditions of early Anglo-Saxon history. As will be seen, the points of contrast between the culture of the three districts in question and that of other districts occupied by the invaders are so strongly marked as to make it instantly recognizable wherever it occurs. They are such, moreover, that they cannot fail to raise the suspicion that, while the other tribes remained untouched by external influences, except by such as were at work within England itself, until the coming of the missionaries, the Jutes, or at least the principal part of them, namely the Cantwaras, came early under the spell of a culture of a far higher order. If that does not suffice to explain all the numerous points of difference, the only other solution can be that they came of other stock than the Angles and Saxons. Fortunately the task of deciding which of these two explanations, or what proportion of both, is necessary to meet the facts of the case is greatly simplified by the wealth of material for study, and the many valuable data obtainable from analogous material on the Continent.

I. *Kent.*

Not much more than half of Kent comes into the picture of the settlements. The numerous cemeteries are confined almost entirely to the eastern end of the county over the areas

covered by the rocks of the Upper Cretaceous system. Westwards the dense forest of the Weald with Romney marshes
on its south-eastern flank barred the road to expansion; only
the northern fringe of the county, where the upper chalk runs
westwards, offered an outlet. It remains, however, a noteworthy
fact that, throughout the pagan period, practically the whole
of the settlers established themselves to the east of the Medway,
and thus formed a compact community with the sea on three
sides and the river Medway and the Weald on the fourth.
Those settlements west of the Medway of which evidence
remains are, with the exception of such as lay immediately
on the opposite bank, rather to be considered as something
apart—a fact in the culture of this county possessing an
archaeological and even wider significance which has perhaps
never been adequately realized. The very position of Kent,
with its extensive sea-board and its proximity to the Continent, rendered it peculiarly liable to be the first spoils in
the conquest of a victorious invading race. Its white cliffs
were the first glimpse of the promised land, and as in the dim
centuries before the Christian era the Brythons dispossessed
the Goidels of it, so in their turn came the Jutes, Romans,
and Normans to seize and hold it for their own. In Kent,
alone of all the districts occupied by the English, there can be
no question of avoidance of Roman roads. Kent stands in this
respect almost by itself: and since the Channel was first formed
in Palaeolithic times, nature has made Kent the gateway of
England, and at the same time has so ordered things that
along the direct line from the point of coast nearest to the
Continent almost to the first fords of the Thames, should
run the bare ridge of the chalk to provide a highway into
England for all time, and one which only the inventions of
modern civilization have dared to supplant. It thus happened
that right through the heart of the lands available for settlement
in Kent ran the main high-road of the Roman road-system,
with several smaller roads branching from its diagonal line
to all the convenient landing-places east and south and
north. So short was the distance from the sea to the

limit of the habitable area, and so closely settled was the land, that for the invaders the Roman roads stood in the same relation to the sea as in other districts existed between any chance tracks and the river from which they led to the high ground. Consequently it is hardly surprising that, given any length of Roman road in Kent, along it should be found cemeteries, often in rapid succession, showing how thoroughly the new-comers must have eradicated all sign of the former inhabitants. Along the main road itself, south-east of Canterbury, lie the cemeteries of Bifrons, Patrixbourne, Beakesbourne, Bishopsbourne, Kingston, Barham, Sibertswold and Dover itself; to the north-west, Faversham, Chatham Lines, and four more before Rochester is reached. Eastwards from Canterbury to Richborough the road passes another line; north-eastwards to Ramsgate lies a third. At the termini of these roads the Romans had established fortresses at Dover(Dubrae), Richborough (Rutupiae), Reculver (Regulbium), Rochester (Durobrivis), while inland was the important town of Durovernum, the modern Canterbury, and a smaller post at Durolevum, probably Faversham. The evidences of Roman occupation are as numerous here as anywhere in England, and the Teutonic cemeteries far outnumber those of any other area of equal extent in this country. Yet in spite of that, the abandonment of the Roman towns in favour of the open country is almost as marked. Outside the walls of three principal towns relics of the Saxon period have, it is true, been found, but they are never of great importance. A small cemetery at Rochester, just outside the line of the Roman enceinte, contained but a few poorly furnished graves, and the same was the case at Dover and also at Canterbury. Among the earliest settlements in Kent were one on Chatham Lines and another at Bifrons, south-east of Canterbury. In each case the invaders seem to have preferred to establish themselves on high ground commanding the town, rather than coop themselves within four walls, which they were totally unqualified by experience to defend. The rivers of Kent are small and of no great value as means of communication, and yet the position of a few cemeteries suggests that neither the Stour nor the Medway was entirely neglected. The earliest area occupied is recorded to have been the Isle of Thanet, given by Vortigern as a place of habitation to Hengist and his followers, whom the former ruler had summoned to aid him against the Picts and Scots. The new-comers evidently did not trust the British, as at the passage of the channel which then separated the Isle of Thanet from the mainland of Kent, their chief early settlement of Sarre stood to guard the approach along the Roman road from Canterbury.

The culture of the Cantwaras as displayed by the discoveries in the cemeteries presents numerous points of absorbing interest, and not the least of these is the presence of two distinct cultures, which can only be ascribed to admixture of race. One of them predominates to an overwhelming degree, but the material also points to early participation in the settlement of Kent by a second tribal element, which at a later period must have been absorbed by the more numerous race. Signs of the second group are but scanty and may be left on one side for the moment. The main culture, on the other hand, stands out in such striking contrast to that of the rest of England that it becomes at once hard to credit that the Cantwaras could ever have been of a race that traced its origins to ancestors of the same stock as the Angles or Saxons proper. That they did so, is one of the difficulties which have to be accounted for, but it may safely be said that the archaeological evidence contains but little warrant for its unqualified acceptance. What then are the chief characteristics of this Kentish culture? It shows in the first place every sign of greater wealth, amounting even to luxury; the race who owned it was evidently in close touch throughout with the chief centres of Teutonic civilization on the Continent and had ready access to the means of developing its art and crafts. Glass vessels are here of almost everyday occurrence; gold is plentiful and in common use, not as elsewhere in England a luxury for the few, and bearing the manifest stamp of fabrication outside of local workshops. In Kent it is employed as a medium for the expression of the strivings of the Kentish craftsmen to evolve a purely native style, semi-barbaric perhaps at its best, but bold in conception and marked by a high degree of technical skill in its execution. The finest Kentish work yields in nothing to the best contemporary productions of the Continental workshops, such as are met with in France and along the line of the southern stream of migration from the shores of the Black Sea. The richness and accuracy of the cloison work, so typical of Kentish jewellery, is unsurpassed, and it is accompanied by a much truer sense of form and a greater repression in design than, for instance, its equivalents among Frankish relics. The second feature of the Kentish culture is the many connexions which it seems to possess with southern rather than northern Germanic art, and here several points call for notice.

(i) The cloison technique has already been mentioned. It only remains to say that the objects on which it first appears in Kent are in point of form those of contemporary France and Germany, not of the rest of England.

(ii) While the Kentish and other English cultures have many forms in common, others which are quite scarce among the latter occur here in considerable numbers. Among these may be noted several brooch forms, such as the varieties with radiate head-plate, whether semicircular or oblong. Certain forms of buckles, especially those with a triangular plate with studs at each angle, the shoe-shaped belt-rivets (fig. 26), perforated spoons, gold pendants set with amethysts or garnets, are all among the almost everyday finds in Kentish graves. The axe, whether the hewing-axe or the true throwing-axe, is met with if but rarely; the *angon*, the long slender throwing-spear, is occasionally found.

(iii) The most marked contrast, however, is to be seen in the pottery. There is nothing here of the half-fired hand-made ware such as was made among Anglian and Saxon tribes. On the contrary, the paste is of a hard gritty texture, far more akin to that of Roman fabrics, and the firing is

good. The chief feature of the Kentish pottery, however, lies
in the fact that it is made on the wheel, so that instead of an in-
finite variety of irregular often misshapen forms, the vase-types,
though few and simple, exhibit in themselves that command
of form and trueness of line which the potter's wheel can
alone ensure. It is not that hand-made vases are entirely
unknown, but such as are thus made are the common ware
which may be found almost anywhere among peoples whose
civilization is not of a very high order. The characteristic
vase-types include three principal varieties—firstly, a bottle-
shaped vase with egg-shaped or spheroidal body, a long neck
and a spreading lip; secondly, a biconical squat form with
clearly defined carination at the middle, a moulded rim, and
sometimes a short, wide mouth; and lastly, a handled jug with
pinched spout. Of this last only a few specimens are known;
more common is the bottle-vase, the most important in many
ways (fig. 19). It is almost exclusively found in the graves
of men. Of thirteen found at Sarre only two specimens came
from graves of women, while two other cases were doubtful.
They seem to be commoner in the earlier cemeteries, such as
Sarre and Chatham Lines. From the enormous total of graves
excavated by Bryan Faussett on the Downs between Canterbury and Dover, he only obtained some four examples, three
of which were associated with warriors' gear. This group of
cemeteries, with the exception of Bifrons on the northern
fringe, represents the period of gradual expansion after the
occupation of Kent had been rendered secure once and for all.
Consequently these bottle-vases furnish an important clue to
the origin of the Kentish settlers, as will be seen in the next
chapter. The decoration of Kentish pottery also differs from
that of other Anglo-Saxon wares; the designs are more often
than not executed by means of a toothed roulette in bands
round the body of the vase, with the occasional use of wooden
stamps to produce stars and the like, such as formed the basis
of ceramic ornament among the Angles and Saxons.

(iv) None of the true Kentish pottery served as urns for
the reception of the ashes of the dead ; in every case it

Fig. 19. Bottle-vases from Kent.

appears as accessory vessels placed along with other objects in inhumation graves. In the typical Kentish cemeteries, cremation is unknown. Whether every significance of the rite had vanished from the minds of the Jutes may be doubtful ; some vestige perhaps of the ideas connoted by it, of purification or of liberation of the soul from the body, still survived in the practice which was so frequently observed by Faussett during his exploration of Kentish graves. More than once he states that the coffin or body showed signs of having 'passed the fire'. In one instance, at Coombe, ashes were found, but that they actually belonged to a cremation burial, is not clear. All the genuine examples of cremation which occur in Kent undoubtedly belong to the second element among the inhabitants, which remains to be dealt with later.

(v) Lastly, the mode of burial seems to differ in certain particulars. It appears to have been quite usual in Kent to heap up a small tumulus over each grave. Possibly this is not peculiar to Kent ; in many other districts agricultural operations may have removed all traces, but at any rate in Kent it seems to coincide with a practice of burying the dead at a greater depth, as a rule 3 ft. or over. In the Anglo-Saxon districts, on the other hand, the usual depth is from $1\frac{1}{2}$ to 2 ft., the greater depths being the exception. The orientation of Kentish graves is remarkably regular ; they almost always point due East and West, with an occasional variation to South-West, the head laid at the western end. This is the direction of about 90 %, the variant orientations, such as South and North, together with those in which no certainty could be arrived at, composing the remainder. Faussett, in the diary of his excavations, constantly refers to the presence of signs of the deceased having been interred in a coffin, of which iron nails or clamps sometimes remained as testimony.

It is hardly a matter for surprise that, with all these marked differences in the Kentish graves, the greater richness of contents, and the numerous signs of constant intercourse with the Continent, it becomes a far easier task to obtain reliable data for constructing a chronological table of types. As usual, a great part of this evidence is furnished by the brooches, but in Kent the typological method is strengthened by the corroborative evidence of coins. Some account of the development of the more distinctive Kentish brooches has been published by Mr. Reginald Smith,[1] but a series of illustrations may help to a better comprehension of the wealth of Kentish material and of the results which can be obtained from the application of this method, as it is only by tabulating a large series of finds that reliable results can possibly be obtained. It might be expected that, in view of the early date to which the historians assign the first landing of the settlers, there would be available quite a large number of finds which could be definitely assigned to the latter part of the fifth century, but as a matter of fact it is by no means easy to fix on any grave as incontestably belonging to that period. By comparison, however, with Continental finds much that would otherwise appear to be largely hypothesis receives full confirmation. Some of this evidence must be left for discussion in the next chapter; other points, however, may be noticed here. For purposes of simplicity, it has been thought well to divide the Kentish graves into four periods, which may be taken to cover a period of fifty years each. Naturally there is a far greater wealth of material for testing the later periods. This is only what might be expected with the influx of additional settlers and the gradual increase of the population. The periods also must not be regarded as hard and fast divisions, hedged off from one another by a sharp line of types. There is necessarily a certain amount of overlap, and this has to be taken into full consideration.

A (A. D. 450–500). The first fifty years after the generally accepted date of the landing of Hengist and Horsa in A. D. 449 just completes the fifth century. There is little reason to suppose that prior to that any effective settlements were established, and certainly there is no archaeological evidence to support such a hypothesis. As typical of this first period, a

---

[1] *Journal of Archaeological Institute*, lxv. 65.

Fig. 20.   Contents of Grave at Chatham Lines, Kent.

grave found by Douglas in 1779 on Chatham Lines furnishes a good example.[1] It is here given in detail.

Below a tumulus, at a depth of 5 ft. and in a cist, lay the skeleton of a woman with head to the South. There was some cause to believe that the body had been originally buried in a coffin. In the grave the following objects were found, disposed at different parts of the body (fig. 20):

(a) Two small gilt-bronze brooches with semicircular heads, three knobs, and simple zig-zag and linear decoration.

(b) Two small brooches with oblong head of similar material and similarly ornamented.

(c) A large iron buckle with tinned bronze plate.

(d) A smaller bronze buckle.

(e) Two small gilt-bronze saucer or 'button' brooches decorated with a rudely executed human face.

(f) A silver spoon with perforated bowl and handle set with garnets in cloisons, laid between the legs.

(g) Small bronze buckle.

(h) Portions of an ivory armlet.

(i) Ten silver ear-rings threaded with eighteen beads of glass, amber, and red paste. These lay by the pelvis.

(j) A piece of fluted bronze.

(k) Various beads of crystal, black glass, amber, red and yellow paste, and black paste with yellow streaks.

There were also found:

(l) Iron knife.

(m) Three perforated coins—(i) of bronze, uncertain, (ii) of silver, Valentinian (A.D. 364-375 or 375-392), and (iii) of silver, Anthemius (A.D. 467-472).

(n) Sherds of pottery.

The coin of Anthemius provides an approximate date or at least a *terminus post quem*, and there is other evidence to show that the ascription of the grave to the first period should be correct. The decoration of the brooches is in the simplest linear designs, such as might be expected at a time when the

---

[1] *Nenia Britannica*, p. 7, Pl. II.

Northern zoomorphic ornament was still in its infancy and
had not made itself felt in the districts to the south. The
brooches with semicircular heads bear in their three knobs
definite signs of a period at which the initial stages in the
development of the type had not entirely vanished. The
earliest brooches of this class known are found on the northern
shores of the Black Sea.[1] In these the two side-knobs form
the terminals of the bar which supported the spring-coil and
at a slightly later stage a third knob of a purely decorative
character is added to the top of the brooch. It is only when
the method of fixing the spring-coil becomes simpler that the
knobs, in losing their functional character, assume a mere ornamental rôle, and that the way is prepared for the addition of
extra knobs, sometimes amounting to as many as ten in
number, all round the edge of the head-plate. With the above
grave-find should be compared another from Chatham Lines,[2]
in which the body lay with the head to the North, accompanied by a similar association of brooch-types, together with
tubular objects of ribbed bronze, probably belt-ornaments,
which recall very vividly certain classes of Roman provincial
work of the latest period. The square-headed brooches from
this grave show the faint beginnings of zoomorphic ornament,
as also in a grave (No. 42) from Bifrons,[3] which is the more
noteworthy as it contained another perforated silver spoon,
with cloison settings, lying also between the thighs and
probably originally suspended from the girdle or laid in the
lap of the deceased. On this occasion a crystal ball in silver
slings lay in the bowl of the spoon, a combination which is
curiously common and the significance of which still remains
a problem. In addition to beads, iron knives, a silver ring
with garnet bezel, and another of plain silver, there were

---

[1] Highly interesting as evidence of the date of this type are the numerous examples from East Prussia, where they represent an early stream of
migration from the south, cut off soon afterwards from further intercourse
with its earlier home by the Slav tribes who in the fifth century harried
Europe and occupied its north-eastern part.

[2] *Nenia Britannica*, p. 23, Pl. VI.

[3] *Arch. Cantiana*, x. 314.

FIG. 21.   OBJECTS FROM GRAVE AT SARRE, KENT.

FIG. 22.   JEWELLED BROOCH WITH ENAMELLED
CENTRE FROM ASH, KENT.

found two square-headed brooches similar to those in the second grave from Chatham Lines, but further decorated with garnets and niello borders, and also two small circular brooches, one of bronze and one of iron, with simple designs executed in garnet cloisons. This is the earliest form of all the cloison brooches, and appears along with others of ornithomorphic form in many early Continental finds. The simple circular type is further dated by the tomb of Childeric, the founder of the Merovingian dynasty (*ob.* 481), discovered at Tournai in 1653. Here, in addition to examples of this brooch type, the tomb-furniture comprised a perfect treasure of objects decorated with cloison work, thus providing valuable evidence for its first appearance in the West. Many of the above-mentioned types pass on into the second period, but it should be noted that apparently none of them was found by Faussett in the numerous graves excavated by him, chiefly on the higher downs.

B (A. D. 500–550). The best example of a grave of this period is one from Sarre, the important settlement in the Isle of Thanet. Its grave-furniture consisted of the following objects (fig. 21) : [1]

(*a*) A perforated silver spoon.

(*b*) A crystal ball in silver slings.

(*c*) Six gold bracteates or pendants, with zoomorphic designs.

(*d*) Two small gilt-bronze square-headed brooches with linear and incipient zoomorphic ornament, and garnet settings.

(*e*) Two larger bronze brooches of similar form exclusively decorated with zoomorphic patterns.

(*f*) A string of beads with which were also strung 2 small circular brooches of billon with 3 wedge-shaped garnets, disposed at equal distances round a central boss of shell or (?) meerschaum.

(*g*) A green bell-shaped glass vase with pointed base and decorated with applied threads.

(*h*) Gold braid, evidently woven into a head-dress.

In addition there were iron knives, keys, and shears, a

---

[1] *Arch. Cantiana*, v. 310 (grave 4).

bronze buckle, shoe-shaped belt-rivets of bronze and silver, a bronze pin or needle, 2 Roman bronze coins and fragments of a comb, and of bronze and silver edging. The evidence furnished by this grave is purely typological, but it may be noted that the square-headed brooch with linear decorations is identical in pattern with one from the second grave at Chatham Lines. The use of zoomorphic ornament is by this time, however, in full swing, and for that reason it should belong to the end rather than the beginning of the period. A new type now appears in the circular brooch with garnet settings. At first small, in keeping with the simplest form of cloison brooches, it later increases in size, a phenomenon which is by no means confined to Kent. All over Saxon England and also on the Continent the later phases of this early Teutonic culture are emphasized by what appears to be the vulgarity in taste so often found among peoples passing from a state of unvarnished semi-barbarism to a so-called civilization. Other evidence in support of this period will be adduced later from the antiquities of the Isle of Wight.

C (A. D. 550–600). The results of Faussett's excavations belong almost entirely to this and the succeeding period and, as a specimen find, the contents of a grave from Kingston Down near Canterbury may be quoted.[1] The body had been buried about 2 ft. deep, in a coffin, but bore no traces of fire. It contained, besides the skeleton—

(a) A circular silver brooch, overlaid with a thin gold plate decorated with filigree, on the outer edge of which were placed three bosses of (?) shell with garnet centres; at the centre was a fourth boss with centre of alternate garnet and blue-stone or glass. From the central boss three triangular rays terminating in small garnet cloisons extend towards the circumference. The type is that of fig. 22, found by Douglas at Ash, between Canterbury and Richborough.[2]

(b) A bronze bracelet with two confronted animal-heads repeated thrice at regular intervals round it.

[1] C. Roach Smith, *Inventorium Sepulchrale*, 91.
[2] *Nenia Britannica*, p. 48, Pl. XII, fig. 1.

(*c*) A circular silver brooch similar to those from the grave at Sarre, but larger and with three long wedge-shaped garnets in the intervening spaces.

(*d*) A pendant of bluish stone or glass in silver setting.

(*e*) Coins of Claudius and Carausius (not of any value for dating).

(*f*) A shell and two earthenware discs.

(*g*) Two ivory double-pointed piercers.

(*h*) A small bronze bell and other miscellanea.

Except the first two, the objects had been placed in a wooden casket of which the fittings only remained. The brooch (*a*) with its four bosses and the filigree ornament, represents the advance in the jeweller's craft which reaches its climax in the succeeding period. The type with wedge-shaped garnets shows a further development during this period in a variety in which step-shaped garnets make their appearance, as a rule associated with a species of knot-pattern, which in reality is a dismembered fragment of an animal-form, in accordance with the apogee of the first period of the zoomorphic style.[1] To this third period belongs much of the glass which forms such a feature of Kentish graves and also a large number of the oval and pear-shaped pendants with cabochon settings, and others of circular form with garnet settings and filigree ornament, which apparently supplanted the true bracteate. A group of pendants was found, associated with Merovingian coins of the fifth to seventh centuries, at Sibertswold Down,[2] and a simple brooch with wedge garnets was accompanied at Gilton by a barbarous copy of a coin of Justinian (A. D. 527–565).[3]

D (A. D. 600–650). The lower limit of this period is quite uncertain, as it depends entirely on how soon the practice of depositing objects with the dead ceased among a converted people. The missionary influence, apart from the set-back caused by Eadbald's relapse about 616, must have been strongly at work for some time before the beginning of the

[1] Cp. Salin, op. cit., p. 239, fig. 537.
[2] *Inv. Sepulchrale*, 131.   [3] Ibid., 16.

seventh century, if the date of Æthelbert's baptism in 597 is
in any way a criterion of the effects of Christian teaching on
the Cantwaras at large.   There is one important consideration
to be taken into account, namely, that in Kent alone do any
examples of the second period of the zoomorphic ornament
occur.   An odd example found outside the county is certainly
Kentish work.   But even in Kent this second style is scarce,
and the major part of the examples known are associated
with the latest development of the cloison brooch or objects
with monograms and signs which seem to indicate the spread
of Christianity.   Had the old burial practices continued
longer, it is certain that with all the manifest signs of close
intercourse with France, a greater amount of material proof
would have been forthcoming from Kentish graves.   This
intercommunication, doubtless initiated in a large measure by
the alliance of Æthelbert with Bertha, a Frankish princess,
and the constant passing to and fro of the missionaries and
delegates sent out by Rome and the Gallic Church, is to be
seen in the presence of typical Frankish buckles and the like,
the frequent finds of glass, probably from Belgian and Rhenish
sources, and the occasional discovery of Merovingian coins.
An approximate date for the limits of the period is further
provided by the highly important grave from Sarre [1] to which
reference has often been made.   Its contents were—

   (a) A large circular gold brooch with five (?) shell and garnet
bosses and two bands of garnet step cloisons, between which
are thin plates of gold with filigree ornament (fig. 23).

   (b) A bronze bowl with open-work foot and, originally, two
drop handles.

   (c) A necklace of glass, glass paste, and pear-shaped amethyst
beads together with five pendants—(i) circular, set with glass-
paste mosaic, (ii–v) gold coins of (1) Mauricius Tiberius (582–
602), (2) imitation of same, of (3) Chlotair (613–628), and
(4) Heraclius (610–641).

   (d) An iron object, somewhat like a sword in form and

[1] *Arch. Cantiana*, iii. 45 ; Pl. II and III.

probably the 'spatha', used in weaving for separating the threads of the warp.[1]

No further development of the above-mentioned brooch is known to archaeology, and its assignment to this period is further strengthened by the finest example known, which was found by Faussett on Kingston Down.[2] This specimen, in addition to the knot-pattern mentioned above, has the pin-catch decorated with the typical animal head, as found throughout the second zoomorphic style. It is, so far as Kent

FIG. 23. CLOISON BROOCH FROM SARRE.

is concerned, an importation from France, where objects have been found on which both this type of animal head and also earlier forms occur concurrently (see fig. 3).[3] It is to this last period that much of the magnificent jewellery from King's Field at Faversham belongs. Thus buckles with 3-knobbed trian-gular plates, in imitation of a common late-Frankish type, are decorated with filigree knot-work zoomorphic patterns, and in one case with a fish, probably used as a Christian emblem.

[1] C. Roach Smith, *Collectanea Antiqua*, vi. 167, fig. 2.
[2] *Inv. Sepulchrale*, 77 (grave 205) and Pl. I.
[3] The first example in the fifth line.

At Faversham, too, appears the Saxon saucer brooch with ornament in which the influence of the wedge-garnet brooches can be clearly traced. Their presence in Kent may be in part due to a back-flow resulting from the spread of Kentish influence in other parts of England to which attention has been drawn, but it is almost certainly also attributable to the presence of another cultural element in the Kentish domain.

In certain cemeteries within the area to which the typical Kentish graves belong, and in those of a group along the shores of the Thames, west of the Medway, this second element can be clearly traced. East of the Medway it is practically confined to the cemeteries of Chatham, Milton near Sittingbourne, Faversham, Sarre, and Ash, all close to the Thames or the scene of the earliest landing. The only cemetery off this line in which it appears to any appreciable extent is Bifrons. It is marked in this eastern group by the presence of certain classes of objects which are otherwise foreign to Kent. They are—

(1) Cruciform brooches. These are more numerous than might be expected.[1] They are, however, invariably of early types; even what is perhaps the most advanced, namely one from Milton, now in Maidstone Museum, has a long pin-catch and loose side-knobs, always early features. At Bifrons one appears in company with a rectangular cloison brooch of simple design.[2]

(2) Annular bronze brooches. These are not common, but at Bifrons two, one of which is identical with many from Anglian and Saxon cemeteries, are similarly associated with a rectangular cloison ornament.[3]

(3) At Milton were also found a simple bronze tab, two facetted attachment-plates, a long belt-plate formed of ribbed tube with a flat projecting flange, and other objects, all identical with specimens from the important Dorchester find.

[1] At least 3 from Bifrons, 2 from Milton, and one each from Faversham and Lyminge, besides other diminutive examples, are known to the writer personally.

[2] *Arch. Cantiana*, x. 305.   [3] Ibid., 304.

Fig. 24. Cinerary Urns of Saxon type from Northfleet, Kent.

Fig. 25. Gold Bracteates from Bifrons and Sarre, Kent.

(4) At Sarre, as mentioned above, and also at Bifrons were found gold bracteates. One from Bifrons is the early type of the leaping man (fig. 25).

(5) Saucer brooches found at Chatham, Faversham, and near Canterbury.

These and allied finds only appear for the most part as intrusive material among the huge mass of typical Kentish relics, but they are all, with the exception of some of the saucer brooches, undoubtedly early, and as such may possibly be productive of important conclusions in the question of origins, as evidence of a mixture of tribal elements. The group of settlements to the west of the Medway is, however, on a somewhat different footing. With the exception, perhaps, of cemeteries on the banks of the Medway itself, there are apparently no signs of the presence of the early distinctive culture of Kent. They seem to mark the presence in this district of an entirely different racial element, more than probably Saxon, and it may well be that such finds as those at Higham, near Rochester, and Northfleet represent early settlements of Saxons advancing up the Thames. Their cemeteries are small in size and consequently cannot have been long in existence. Possibly later their inhabitants moved further westwards under pressure of Kentish expansion or were exterminated by their Kentish neighbours. In the cemeteries of Higham and Northfleet early specimens of saucer brooches appear, but more important is the presence of hand-made pottery of the typical Anglian and Saxon fabric (fig. 24). At Northfleet this pottery had served to hold the ashes of cremated dead. This clear evidence of cremation at this point of the Thames valley is of the highest importance. It links these cemeteries with those of Croydon and Mitcham further west, and as the rite is unknown elsewhere in Kent, except for a few Saxon urns found at Hollingbourne near Maidstone,[1] it is only capable of the interpretation offered above. At Horton Kirby, one of the cemeteries in the trans-Medway group, there were found associated with a burial,

---

[1] And one other at Folkestone, *V. C. H.*, *Kent*, i. 364.

not only a typical Saxon pot but also a handled flagon such as is well known from late Romano-British interments in Kent.[1] The practice of including Romano-British objects in a grave may as a rule be taken as a sign of early date.

II. *Isle of Wight.*

The archaeology of this period in the Isle of Wight presents some very interesting problems, by reason of its almost complete contradiction of the records of the historians, subsequent to that which concerns the first settlement, as given by Bede in the passage quoted at the beginning of the chapter. The island next appears in history in A.D. 530 when, according to the Anglo-Saxon Chronicle, it was overrun by the West Saxons under Cerdic, with great slaughter of its existing occupiers at Withgarasbyrig, and handed over by Cerdic to Withgar. It is not heard of again until A.D. 681, at which date Bede records that Wulfhere of Mercia gave to Æthelwalch of Sussex, on the occasion of the latter's baptism, the two provinces of 'Wight and the land of the Meonwaras, which last is in the realm of the West Saxons'. In A.D. 685 Ceadwalla of Wessex slew Æthelwalch and conquered Wight, which until then had been 'entirely given over to heathenism'. The points to be noticed in these bare accounts are, firstly, that from Bede's entry of the year 681 it might be inferred that the Isle of Wight at that date did not belong to the West Saxons. If this was so, at some time between 530 and 681 it must have passed into the possession of Wulfhere or others, though it is difficult to understand how the Meonwara district, lying between the Isle of Wight and the important Saxon town of Winchester, remained West Saxon. Secondly, that the time given for the continuance of pagandom in the island is a very extended one, only comparable with that of Sussex, and apparently, from Bede's entry of 685, somewhat closely connected with it. Professor Oman, indeed, infers from the events of

[1] For knowledge of this find and of the Hollingbourne urns the writer is indebted to Mr. H. Elgar of the Maidstone Museum.

685 that the Isle of Wight had no connexion with the
West Saxons, and adduces in support of this contention
the conversion of the Saxons some forty years previously, and
also the fact that the Isle of Wight had a different royal
house to that of the Saxons, which Ceadwalla endeavoured to
exterminate by the slaughter of Arwald, the king, and his two
brothers. If then the history contradicts itself, what light
can archaeology offer?

Three cemeteries are known, all along the central chalk
ridge which divides the island in two. They are, in order
from East to West, Arreton Down, Bowcombe Down, and
Chessel Down, the last by far the most important. There
and at Arreton Down graves were found in barrows; at
Bowcombe Down some were uncovered in a large Bronze Age
barrow. The Bowcombe Down finds were not numerous,
consisting mainly of weapons and bronze buckles; at Arreton
Down an iron axe was recovered. In 1855, 150 graves were
explored at Chessel Down in addition to others opened in
1818.[1] From them was obtained a fine series of relics, which
from an archaeological standpoint are of the highest importance, by reason of the fact that they are almost exclusively
Jutish in character. The number of objects which can with
any degree of plausibility be called Saxon constitutes a
quite infinitesimal proportion of the whole. Square-headed
brooches of Kentish type, sometimes set with garnets, others
of simple circular cloison and ornithomorphic form, Kentish
forms of the buckle, jewelled spoons, crystal pendants, shoe-
shaped rivets and other objects, are all reminiscent of what is
found elsewhere only in Kent. But in all this similarity
there are two points particularly to be noticed, firstly the
predominance among the brooches of one variety, the square-
headed type, and secondly the absence of the later Kentish
jewelled types. The former may perhaps be regarded merely
as a local peculiarity, in part due to the isolation of the Jutish
community which established itself in the Isle of Wight. For
the absence of the latter, however, some further explanation

[1] G. Hillier, *History and Antiquities of the Isle of Wight*, p. 59.

is necessary. Some 20 of the Jutish square-headed type
are known, and practically all are ornamented with simple
linear patterns. Unfortunately it is impossible to test this
important group according to associated finds. Hillier, in his
account of the finds, only records the contents of one grave
of interest, but these may be given in detail, as they offer
valuable points of comparison with contemporary Kentish
graves. The grave contained a burial by inhumation, with
which were associated—

(*a*) Three gilt-bronze square-headed brooches with simple
linear design.

(*b*) A bronze equal-armed brooch ; the ends being semicircular, radiated, and set with garnets.

(*c*) A small circular bronze brooch with three wedge-shaped
garnets.

(*d*) An iron *spatha,* as in the grave from Sarre(*supra,*p .112).

(*e*) A bronze (?) key, bronze buckle, and iron knife.

(*f*) A silver perforated spoon set with garnets, in which
lay—

(*g*) A haematite ball in silver slings.

(*h*) One bronze-bound bucket and two bronze frames of
similar buckets.

The combination of (*a*) and (*c*) is identical with that in
graves from period *B* in Kent, so that this piece of evidence
suggests an early sixth-century burial. On the one side,
quite a large number of somewhat later pieces came from this
cemetery, a fact which seems to suggest that the settlement
to which it belonged retained its Jutish character for some
little time after the date given for Cerdic's slaughter of the
inhabitants. On the other side, the number of objects of
the nature of Saxon workmanship is exceedingly small. Two
large bronze square-headed brooches, one of which, in view of
the recent Alfriston finds, suggests Sussex as its origin, while
the other is of late sixth or even seventh-century type : a few
cremation-urns and other unimportant objects are all that
in any way suggest an admixture of Saxon culture. It is,
however, impossible to say what proportion of the male

population may or may not have been Saxon, without careful investigation of skeletal remains, as the graves of warriors bear a close resemblance to one another all over England. Consequently there exists a possibility that the record in the Chronicle is true, to the extent that the male element was practically exterminated by a Saxon raid, while the Jutish women were spared as the spoils of victory. There still remains the difficulty presented by the record of the extermination of a royal house in 681. Unless much archaeological material still exists as yet undiscovered, the inferences to be drawn from what is at present known of the culture of the island seem to point to a period of absolute insignificance. Otherwise it is difficult to explain the total absence of relics which would serve to bridge over the interval of nearly a century between the limits of the existing evidence and the termination of the period during which the inhabitants had been entirely ' given over to heathenism '.

III. *The Land of the Meonwaras.*

The exact area denoted by this name is uncertain, though, in view of the dense forest with which the part of Hampshire west of Southampton Water was covered, it is probable that it refers only to the eastern side of the county north of Portsmouth, that is to say in the vicinity of the Meon valley itself. It is curious, therefore, that the only cemetery known from this district is a small one at Droxford in the valley of the Meon. The diagnosis of the character of the relics from this cemetery given in the account of the Anglo-Saxon relics in the *Victoria County History for Hampshire*,[1] and recently quoted in an article on the English Settlements,[2] may perhaps be questioned. Though simple, they would seem to be in the main Jutish, though here too, as perhaps is only natural, there are signs of some intercourse with Sussex. An instance is a saucer brooch which has hitherto been regarded as West

---

[1] Vol. i. 379.

[2] R. Lennard, in Hoops' *Reallexikon der germanischen Altertumskunde* (*Englisches Siedelungswesen*), p. 603.

Saxon, but which should, by reason of certain details in the decorative design, be regarded rather as of South Saxon origin. The cemetery evidently did not remain very long in use, so that here, as in the Isle of Wight, there exists a blank in the culture which archaeology is unable to explain. One further point alone remains to be noticed, namely the proximity of Winchester to this district. If the town was not sacked in an earlier raid, it is surely rather to this group of settlers than to the West Saxons that its fall must be ascribed.

CHAPTER VII

THE ORIGIN OF THE JUTES

A RECENT writer on the vexed question of the origin of the Jutes sums up the arguments as follows: 'To the present writer it seems that whilst the evidence upon which Bede based his statement that the Iutae dwelt north of the Angles *may* have been insufficient, the evidence by which it is sought to refute this statement indubitably *is* insufficient, and that Bede's statement accordingly holds the field.' Thus a writer (the italics are his) approaching the problem from the side of history and philology. The question remains, however, Are all the sources of information therewith exhausted? Certainly, in the above expression of opinion no account whatever is taken of archaeology, nor does the evidence to be derived from this quarter ever seem to have met with the treatment which its very intricacy demands. Can archaeology throw any light on the subject of the origin of this branch of the English settlers? It would be strange if it could not render some assistance, however small, when it is able to offer such clear evidence of the sources of the other divisions of the Anglo-Saxon culture.

The statement of Bede referred to in the above quotation is to be found in the 15th chapter of his 1st Book, where he describes the homeland of the Angles as being 'inter provincias Iutarum et Saxonum'. As there seems to be no shadow of doubt that the Angles lived north of the Saxons and in the Danish Peninsula, it follows that, in Bede's estimation at least, the Jutes must have occupied the part of the peninsula still further north, or the modern Jutland.[1] The question of the apparently greater affinity of the Kentish

---

[1] Or possibly the small portion of the peninsula in which the Frisian dialect still survives (see p. 81).

dialect (such little as is known of it) to the language of
Friesland as compared with that of Jutland is the stumbling-
block which has increased the difficulties in the way of solving
the problem in a straightforward manner.   A concise statement of the various explanations offered is to be found in
Mr. R. W. Chambers's edition of 'Widsith', from which the
quotation at the beginning of the chapter is derived.[1]   The
dialects of England in Anglo-Saxon times have all been
shown to belong to a language-group whose distribution
ranges from the mouth of the Rhine, or more strictly speaking
Friesland, to Schleswig-Holstein.   The distinction according
to which the languages of north and central Europe have
been divided into an East and a West Germanic group seems
to call for a modification in favour of a simpler and more
natural division of a Northern and a Southern group.   The
line of demarcation between the two groups is, for the period
here in question, curiously sharply defined.   It corresponds
with one of the narrowest parts of the Danish peninsula,
which in turn is practically identical with the modern
frontier between Germany and Denmark.   The area immediately to the north, the modern Jutland, may perhaps be
regarded as debatable country, as it is not improbable
that prior to the westward migration of the tribes inhabit-
ing the Peninsula, the Low-German group of languages
extended slightly beyond the line above mentioned, but
that eventually the Danish peoples, forced southward by
the Swedish groups, occupied all the territory northward
of the line, and thus instituted what has practically remained fast to the present time as a firm barrier between
the northern and southern linguistic divisions of the Germanic races.   From the side of language, therefore, it is
within the bounds of the southern division that the home
of the Jutes is to be sought.   This division, however, is
one of very wide extent, covering as it does the whole area
occupied by tribes speaking all the various shades of Teutonic
speech, from the Low-German of North Germany and Holland

[1] p. 240.

—to the High—German of South Germany, Austria, and other parts of Central Europe. If the Jutes sprang from this pure Low-German stock, then it is within the stretch of country between the Zuider Zee and Kiel that one would naturally expect to find the sources of the Kentish culture indicated by the presence of similar archaeological material. The question to be answered in the rest of this chapter is, 'Is this so, and if not, whence did the Kentish culture come?'

First of all, then, how do the finds from Kent, the Isle of Wight, and South Hampshire compare with those of the two Continental regions in which the majority of historians and philologists would place the Jutes, according as the one or other set of arguments weighs most heavily with them, the two areas in question being Jutland and Friesland.

In the last chapter it was noted that within the archaeological material from Kent, two distinct elements could be traced, the one characterized by cloison jewellery, glass, and wheel-made pottery, the other represented by objects such as might easily have been found in the Anglo-Saxon districts. This is exclusive of the little group of finds west of the Medway which, as it has been shown, may probably be regarded as Saxon pure and simple. But to assign even the relics from cemeteries to the east of the Medway to any particular part of the North German area, from which the Saxon or Anglian cultures were divided, is a task practically amounting to impossibility. It may perhaps be surmised that some of them came from fairly far north, as for example some little bronze belt-plates from Bifrons,[1] decorated with zoomorphic designs. These bear a somewhat close resemblance to one from Bornholm.[2] But as this island lies outside the area assigned by the historians to the forefathers of the English race, this parallel only serves to demonstrate more forcibly the impossibility above noted. Thus far, then, the problem is no nearer to solution. Is there, then, any other element which possesses a distinctly northern *facies*? Among

---

[1] *Arch. Cantiana*, vii. 313 (Sarre, grave 133).

[2] Sophus Müller, *Ordning*, ii, fig. 505.

the most noticeable objects found in Kent the bracteates (fig. 25) and their kinsmen the jewelled pendants must take a high position. Nothing like the jewelled pendants is known from Bede's homeland of the Jutes, or indeed from any part of North Germany, but that is not the case with the bracteates proper. Among those found in Kent two types are particularly noteworthy, namely that decorated with the figure of a leaping man, of which possibly that from Bifrons[1] is the one solitary representative, and a second type of which several examples are known. The design on this consists of an entwined animal-figure, assigned by Salin to a late period of his Style I.[2] As will be shown later, however, it is more than likely that this type came into being somewhat earlier than Salin would allow. Certainly the associated grave-finds in Kentish grave-fields would seem to call for a somewhat earlier date. The 'leaping man' type is otherwise known from Hanover, Denmark, South Norway, and Sweden,[3] and Salin has remarked that the better examples are found in the south, while in those from further north a carving technique takes the place of the more highly skilled repoussé method of production. This change can only be regarded as a sign of degeneracy, thus arguing for a Southern origin for the type as a whole. And the Kentish example must be reckoned among the latter rather than among the former. The other type belongs to a class which has a somewhat wider distribution, and in Kent is best represented by examples from Bifrons and Sarre. Those from the former cemetery come from the same grave as the 'leaping man' type already mentioned, while the Sarre examples, with one exception, belong to the notable grave which was described in detail in the last chapter, as an example of period B (A.D. 500–550). If, however, Salin is correct in his estimation of the age of this class of bracteate, the grave must be dated to the end of the sixth century, and in that case the bracteates

---

[1] *Arch. Cantiana*, x., fig. on p. 310.
[2] Op. cit., pp. 241–2.
[3] *Antikvarisk Tidskrift för Sverige*, xiv. 44 and 101.

provide a *terminus post quem* of the same nature as *B* coins. Against this, however, must be reckoned the early character of all the other objects in this grave and their close resemblance to those from other graves, both in Kent and the Isle of Wight, where there are no bracteates to complicate matters,—to which must be added the opinion held by philologists that all intercourse between England and Denmark had ceased before the end of the sixth century.[1]

Apart from these two classes of objects, namely the cruciform brooches and other relics of an Anglo-Saxon type, and the bracteates themselves, there is practically nothing in the Kentish culture which warrants the derivation of the so-called Jutish settlers in England from Friesland, North Germany, or from Jutland itself. From the first-mentioned class of relics no exact deductions of any kind can be drawn, and the bracteates by themselves certainly do not justify any hypothesis that the Danish peninsula was responsible for the whole of the marvellous wealth displayed by the finds from Kentish grave-fields. And why is this so? It is necessary to return at this point to the general considerations set forth in the first chapter. It was there demonstrated that, in studying the culture of the Teutonic races of the Continent, it is possible to distinguish between a northern and southern line of migrations, which present marked differences in the cultures of the races which participated in them. The style of culture associated with the northern line is that which is represented by the objects found in the Saxon and Anglian territories in England and the corresponding homelands along the Continental shores of the North Sea. With this culture the majority of the relics found in the Jutish districts of England have nothing in common. Nothing comparable to the masses of jewelled ornaments has ever been found in Northern Europe. The island of Gotland is the only place in the North which, at the period at which the migrations began, had learnt the art of decorating brooches and the like with garnets, and it

[1] e. g. M. G. Clarke, *Side-lights on Teutonic History during the Migration Period*, p. 8.

is hardly possible to go so far afield as the centre of the
Baltic for the origin of one section of the English race.
When cloison jewellery does appear in any quantity, it is
in Scandinavia, and at a time when, as has already been
surmised on other than archaeological grounds, all intercourse, so far as migration at any rate between Northern
Europe and England is concerned, had ceased. In Jutland,
as elsewhere in Denmark, graves of this period were for a long
time unknown. The island of Bornholm alone has produced
graves with rich grave-furniture. But many graves here, as
also in the island of Fünen and in Jutland, are without relics
of any kind. Others in Jutland are described as rather
uncharacteristic and very poorly furnished.[1] Any affinities
which they may possess to other cultures are closest to the
Anglian section of English antiquities. North Germany and
Schleswig-Holstein have been claimed by the Saxons and
Angles. Friesland alone has produced something akin to the
twofold culture observable in Kent, but in Friesland it is the
Anglo-Saxon side that predominates, while in Kent the exact
reverse is the case. What then is the next most probable
source? The mind naturally reverts to the curious passage
in Adam of Bremen [2] on which is based the theory of an
Anglo-Saxon occupation of Brabant, and the equally myste-
rious *Lex Angliorum et Werinorum*, which has given rise to
so many conjectures about the reasons for the presence of
a section of the English settlers round the mouth of the
Rhine. As the map on page 88 shows, the archaeological
evidence for the accuracy of these conjectures lies in the fact
that at one period an undoubtedly Frankish element had
occupied districts to the north of the Rhine in modern
Brabant, Drenthe, and perhaps so far north as Gelderland
and even Friesland itself.

It may here be said at once that it is in Frankish territory
that the origin of most of the Kentish culture must be sought.
The only question is in what particular part of that territory.

---

[1] S. Müller, *Nordische Altertumskunde*, ii. 185 and 191.

[2] *Mon. Germ. hist. Script.* 7. 285 (Ed. Lappenberg, i. 3).

The natural idea, perhaps, in view of the passages mentioned, is to turn to the parts nearest the mouth of the Rhine, namely North Belgium. There is much indeed there that might easily have come from the grave of a Kentish man or woman, but not everything. Many of the earliest cemeteries in Belgium, for example those of Furfooz, Samson, and Spontin, have produced bronze rings, attachment-plates, and the like, such as commonly occur in the North German cemeteries and have also been found at Dorchester, Croydon, and Milton near Sittingbourne. The same cemeteries, none of which extend beyond the middle of the sixth century, have yielded many fine specimens of glass, radiate and bird brooches and other and simple types not unlike the earliest Kentish forms. The oval bronze buckles, the variegated beads and wheel-made pottery are also not wanting. In short, at first sight Belgium would seem to satisfy many of the conditions required. There are, however, certain facts to be remembered in connexion with Belgium. Firstly, practically all the important cemeteries lie to the south of Brussels and mostly in the now thickly populated districts round Charleroi and Namur. Of the three early cemeteries mentioned above, Samson lies on the Meuse between Namur and Huy, Spontin on a small tributary some distance to the south, while Furfooz is situated on another small tributary a short distance south of Dinant. That is to say all these cemeteries lie within an enclave in the heart of Belgium, and thus well away from the main routes of migration. They represent, in fact, the earliest home of the Salian Franks who subsequently swarmed forth over the whole of northern France. Such pressure as was brought to bear on them from the north tended to drive them further southwards, and the whole history of the Frankish occupation of northern France demonstrates beyond a doubt that these inhabitants of Belgium were only held back so long as the decaying power of Rome in Gaul was able to present a sufficiently stout front against the ever-insistent attacks of this powerful confederation. In this inland district they lay secure from,

and untroubled by the pressure which was ever threatening
their Teutonic kinsmen occupying districts further east along
the main routes of migration. It is on such a line that the
main bulk of the Kentish settlers are to be found—and that
the Rhine itself—and in the territory of the Ripuarian Franks.
In his instructive map of the diffusion of the divisions of
Germanic speech, Behagel has assigned to a group, to which
he gives the name of *Westmitteldeutsch*, that part of the
Rhine valley which is now occupied by the Rhineland, and
Hesse-Nassau, that is to say, all the territory lying roughly
within a triangle at whose corners now stand the towns of
Düsseldorf, Frankfurt, and Trier. But not the whole of this
area comes into question in dealing with the origin of the
Kentish settlers. Indeed, it is probably only a small section
of it and that the most northerly, and therefore the nearest
to the sea. This area lies along the Rhine between Coblenz
and Düsseldorf, stretching eastwards into the Eifel district,
together with a narrow strip on the opposite bank. It is
represented by cemeteries such as Meckenheim, Nettersheim,
Kärlich, Kruft, Niederbreisig, Niederdollendorf on the right
bank, and last, and by no means least, Andernach. In this
group of cemeteries there can be found practically every
single constituent that goes to make up the earliest culture
of the Kentish cemeteries. Great care has to be observed
to distinguish between the earlier and later graves in the
cemeteries of this district, and even greater care in dis-
tinguishing the elements due to variant cultures in the Rhine
valley. This latter task, however, has been greatly simplified
by the work of Schliz on the question, so far as it concerns
the Alemannic cemeteries of Rhenish Hesse, Baden, and
Würtemberg.[1] As he is careful to note any intrusive
elements from the Frankish side, it is possible on the other
hand to distinguish with some degree of certainty the Alemannic factors in the Frankish culture of the middle Rhine-
valley. From the time of the withdrawal of the Legion from

---

[1] *Historischer Verein Heilbronn, Bericht* (1900–1903), Heft 7, 1 ff., and
Fundberichte aus Schwaben, xi (1903), 21 ff.

Cologne in 405 and the final occupation of Trier (Augusta Treverorum) by the Franks in A.D. 464, there was a fierce struggle between the Franks and Alemanni for the mastery over the Rhineland, which ended in the victory of the Franks at Zülpich in 496. The early line of division between the two tribes seems to coincide roughly with a line drawn along the Main westwards through Mainz to Luxemburg. In the sixth century the Franks became masters of a considerable district south of this line, as evidenced by the presence of the characteristically Frankish ending of place-names in -heim, side by side with the -ingen or -angen of the Alemanni. It is interesting to note that Schliz more than suspects the participation of provincial Roman artisans in the production of most of the earlier Teutonic objects from the Rhine valley. Among the Alemanni he considers, for instance, the industry of inlaying iron with silver to have originally lain in the hands of the numerous Roman captives. This would account for much that speaks for a survival of late Roman art in this region, always subordinated, however, to the demands of Teutonic masters. At the same time it affords a weighty corroboration of the evidences of similar survivals in certain districts of Saxon England.

Two typical cemeteries of the earlier Frankish period in the Rhineland are those of Andernach (Kirchberg) and of Rittersdorf, Kreis Bitburg, a little north of Trier. That of Andernach is contiguous with the Roman burying-ground, and like the Rittersdorf cemetery shows a transition of types in use from the preceding period of the Roman occupation of the district. These and other early cemeteries present certain marked features which are of great importance for comparison with those of Kent. It may be noted in passing that the almost universal orientation is West to East ; it is not a matter of great import whether the Franks were Christians in the fifth century, and the Jutes at the time of the occupation of Kent were not. It may be fairly assumed that what had been the custom in the land the Kentish settlers had left, the same would they carry on at first in their new home. It is rather to the contents of the graves that attention should be directed. Firstly, from the women's graves come brooch-types such as are associated with early Kentish graves, the principal type being the cloison brooch, either of plain circular or of simple rosette form.[1] As was shown in the last chapter, this is undoubtedly one of the earliest types found in Kent. Further, there are various types of radiate brooches, all comparatively common ; those with semicircular heads are found both with the straight-sided foot and also with the oval foot. The former, which, as Salin has observed, contains in its structure elements derived from a Roman prototype, is well represented in all Frankish cemeteries, but the latter is typically South German. It is certainly strange that this particular type does not occur in Kent, the more so as it is often found decorated with 'Kerbschnitt' patterns, indicating an early period. But a very fine example from Rut-landshire points beyond a doubt to some intercourse, however casual, with this part of Europe. The absence of this type is, however, balanced by other varieties with the oval foot, decorated also with ' Kerbschnitt' or by similar early designs.[2]

More important, however, are the ornithomorphic brooches and certain square-headed varieties as at Kärlich, near Andernach, and at Rittersdorf. In almost every case these are decorated with simple linear ornament such as marks the earlier specimens from Kent and the Isle of Wight. The outstanding difference is the absence of the garnet cloisons. Their presence in many Kentish examples may, however, be regarded as an early expression of the taste for cloison jewellery which eventually becomes the hall-mark of the English Jutish goldsmith's work. There is, however, one type, only repre-sented in the Rhenish cemeteries by isolated examples, which offers an important clue, namely the circular brooch set with four wedge-shaped garnets arranged in a cruciform pattern

[1] These are clearly recognized by Continental archaeologists as belong-ing to the Frankish culture of the fifth century, e. g. Schliz, *Historischer Verein Heilbronn*, loc. cit., p. 11.

[2] e. g. *V. C. H., Kent*, i. 360, Pl. 2, fig. 315. Cp. an example from Niederselters, *Westdeutsche Zeitschrift*, xviii, Pl. 10, fig. 1.

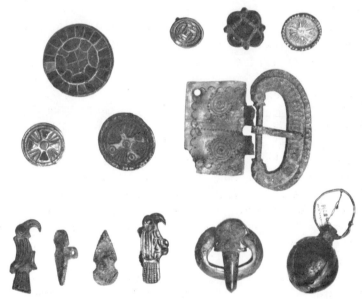

FIG. 26. EARLY FRANKISH BROOCHES, ETC.,
FROM ANDERNACH, GERMANY.

(fig. 26). It was noted in the last chapter that the early examples from Jutish cemeteries, as in the grave from Chessel Down, in the Isle of Wight (p. 118), are always small as compared with the later specimens which are the commonest type found in Kent. It can hardly be a coincidence that it should be in these German cemeteries that the small variety of this type should occur, and, as will be seen later, its presence there is on all fours with other peculiar classes of objects. An unmistakable link with the Rhine districts is a bronze ewer from Wheathampstead, Hertfordshire,[1] of a type which is unknown from other parts of the Continent.

Noteworthy, too, are the beads. The predominant feature of those from early Frankish graves is their relatively small size as compared with the larger and somewhat vulgar beads of the later period. Among the former are to be seen paste beads of all colours—for example, spheroidal forms in bright yellow, red, red with white chain pattern, white with the same design in blue, and cylindrical beads in yellow and red, sometimes with green or black added, while occasionally there are found in Kentish graves beads with *milleflori* patterns, such as occur but rarely indeed in the Frankish cemeteries of the Rhine but are well represented in Alemannish graves, for example as Gammertingen.[2] More important than all these, however, is the occurrence in Kentish graves of pear-shaped beads of amethyst. Only two or three are, as a rule, found in any one grave, demonstrating that they were evidently valued somewhat highly. And it is thus that they occur in Rhenish graves, more often than not used as pendants to a necklace. It may be questioned whether they were not originally obtained as plunder from Roman graves, as they seem to have been much in vogue as pendants to ear-rings and other late-Roman jewellery. Their original source was more than likely Egypt, where amethyst beads were in use from the very earliest times, though the pear-shaped type appears to belong more particularly to the period of Roman occupation.

---

[1] *V. C. H., Herts.*, i. Pl. facing p. 253, fig. 2.
[2] I. W. Gröbbels, *Der Reihengräberfund von Gammertingen*, Pl. xvii.

There is, however, a faint possibility that the material for some of those found in the Rhine district was obtained locally.[1]

Another outstanding feature of Rhenish graves is the wealth of glass vessels of almost every conceivable form that they have yielded to the excavator. During the period of Roman occupation, the Rhine valley was one of the chief centres of glass production in the whole empire. In the various museums in the Rhine valley the Roman glass forms one of their most attractive exhibits, and the fall of the Empire in this district fortunately did not involve the extinction of this important industry. The victorious Teutonic tribes were clearly alive to the desirability of glass vases and the like, and to that end seem to have fostered the industry, although the articles produced under their supervision bear the stamp of their own peculiar artistic taste. Great variety of form is observable in the Frankish glass, but little of it carries on any Roman tradition. The most important types are the simple round-bottomed 'tumbler'; a peculiar waisted beaker with rounded base often terminating in an excrescent knob, and tall conical vases decorated with threads encircling the neck, and other threads below disposed apparently to reproduce the appearance of fluting. Most distinctive of all, however, are beakers with hollow pendent excrescences, somewhat resembling an elephant's trunk. All these and other forms found in this district are to be seen in collections from Kentish cemeteries, which are particularly rich in glass as compared with other parts of England. It is only those counties lying in closest proximity to Kent, such as Sussex, that have produced any quantity of glass, and it is evident that in the districts outside Kent it is quite an exotic. Turning for a moment to the graves of men, it is noticeable that the sword is more characteristic of the earlier Frankish graves. Only in the later period does the broad 'scramasax' appear to have come into general use. This would account for its absence in Kent, and the find of no less than 26 swords in 272

---

[1] B. Stürtz, *Das Rheindiluvium talwärts von Bingerbrück* (*Verhandl. d. Naturhist. Vereins der preuss. Rheinlande u. Westfalens, 67. Jahrg., 1907*).

graves at Sarre. As in Kent, so in the Rhineland, the
'angon', with its small head and exceedingly long shaft, as
well as the axe, whether it be the 'francisca', the throwing-
axe, or the broad hewing-axe, are comparatively speaking
uncommon, and thus the scarcity of these typical Frankish
weapons in Kent need occasion no surprise. What is
found, however, is a peculiar spear with a long slender shaft,
(the head varies in size), and this type is not unknown in
Kent.[1] The shoe-shaped belt-rivets also occur in the Rhineland (fig. 26). So far, then, links between Kent and the
Rhineland are not wanting, although there is admittedly
much that might well have come from other parts of the
Continent occupied by Frankish tribes. The product of the
Kentish cemeteries which would appear, however, to clinch
the argument here offered for a Rhenish source for the
Jutish culture is the pottery. It was noted in the last
chapter that the pottery found in Kent differs from that
yielded by the cemeteries of the Saxon and Anglian districts
of England in being wheel-made. It is this fact that would
seem to constitute the most weighty argument against the
derivation of the Jutish culture as a whole either from Jutland
or Friesland. As already noted, throughout the whole of the
stretch of country from Denmark to Holland native wheel-
made pottery of this date is *never* found ; such pottery,
represented by a fair number of examples in Holland and
Westphalia, where at various periods Frankish tribes held
districts on the outskirts of the Saxon lands, is always
Frankish. On the one hand it is incredible that had the Jutes
come from Jutland, no wheel-made pottery should ever have
been found there, and on the other hand that the Danish types
should never have been found in Kent. The few urns of North
German type from Kentish graves were shown to belong to a
small group of cemeteries which most probably must be ascribed
to a Saxon element living west of the Medway. So far as the
wheel-made vases found in Holland are concerned, these too
may represent a foreign element, namely those Franks who

[1] *Arch. Cantiana*, vii, Pl. XIV.

were eventually driven out by the Saxons, as may be gathered from the passages in Zosimus and Adam of Bremen, who speak of the activities of the latter people in the Netherlands.

The Frankish pottery found there consists exclusively of bi-conical urns, such as also occur in Kent, but this is not the only type known from that county. In the early cemetery of Sarre there appears another form of pottery, namely the bottle-shaped vase mentioned in the last chapter (fig. 19), and it is this ceramic type which, in connexion with all the other objects which could be shown to have been with a high degree of probability derived from the Rhine district, renders it possible to arrive at a certain conclusion of the accuracy of this hypothesis. The specimens illustrated (fig. 27), now preserved in the Provinzial-Museum at Bonn, have been selected from some twenty-four examples in that museum, as typical of the varieties of these bottle-vases from cemeteries of the Rhineland. Their identity with those found in Kent becomes self-evident if they are compared with those illustrated in the last chapter or with others from Sarre figured in *Archaeologia Cantiana*, vii, Plate X. In the Rhine district they occur most commonly in the early cemeteries in the Eifel district and round Andernach, but a few examples also have been found southwards to the Main and beyond.

At Sarre, and apparently also at Andernach, they have been in almost every case found in the graves of men.[1] At Sarre, out of 13 examples, 9 come from graves of men, 2 from those of women, and one is doubtful. Only 4 specimens occurred amongst all the graves excavated by Bryan Faussett, and of these 3 come from men's graves. In the Kirchberg cemetery at Andernach the indications on this point are not so clear, but it was noticed that many of the graves had been plundered. In the Burgtor cemetery, however, one if not two out of three were found with men, the other is doubtful. This latter cemetery is of later date than that at Kirchberg, but their occurrence there merely argues

---

[1] A good example is a grave from Chatham Lines, sketched with the relics in position. It is figured in *Nenia Britannica*, Pl. I.

FIG. 27. BOTTLE-VASES FROM THE RHINELAND.

some persistence of the type, as in Kent.[1] For the most part
they came from cemeteries in which other early relics have
been found, and are thus comparable to some extent with the
handled jugs with trefoil-mouth of which numerous examples
were discovered at Rittersdorf, associated with early cloison
and other brooches. The date of these jugs is clearly determined by the fact that they and other pottery from that
cemetery carry on the tradition of ceramic types recovered
from the latest Roman deposits at Trier, that is to say, of the
early part of the fifth century.

Such then are the chief points of parallelism existent
between the relics of the Rhine valley and those of the Jutish
cemeteries in England. Several others exist, one of which,
namely the curious perforated spoons, can hardly be passed
over. They are by no means unknown in the Rhine valley.
The significance of those from Jutish graves in England is
quite uncertain, but their history seems to throw back to late
Roman spoons, often engraved with monograms, Christian and
otherwise, or with dedicatory inscriptions such as have been
found in the earliest Teutonic graves of the upper Rhine-
valley.[2] Similar coincidences are observable at almost every
point of inquiry, but it is hardly necessary to give a detailed
list of them. The parallelism is, however, so strong that it
seems to call for some attempt to reconcile the antipathetic
factors in the problem of the origin of the Jutes. On the one
side stand the historians demanding a Danish source, and the
philologists divided amongst themselves as to the relative
claims of Jutland and Friesland to that honour ; on the other
stands the evidence derived from archaeology, which denies
the possibility that the bulk of the Kentish settlers can have
owned either of those two countries as their motherland.

[1] In connexion with what has been said above about Belgium, the writer
has only noted one example of this type of vase in the collections at Brussels, Charleroi, Namur, and Liège. It is not figured by Barrière Flary
in his *Arts industriels des Barbares*, though rare examples do occur in
France.

[2] Cp. *Historischer Verein Heilbronn, Bericht* (1900–1903), p. 25. Inter-
mediate forms are figured by Lindenschmit, *Die Altertümer der Merovin-
gischen Zeit*, i, Pl. XXV.

The probable solution of these conflicting claims lies, as so often happens, in a compromise. For the Jutland theory— omitting archaeology for the moment—the witnesses are Bede and possibly also the genealogy of the Jutish royal family. The linguistic evidence would seem rather to favour Friesland, though Jutland does not lack her champions. Among the traditions hovering round Friesland is that tantalizing fragment of the Finn saga[1] containing the obscure mention of a people called the Eotena, and a recital of the deeds of one Hengist the lieutenant of Hnaef in his battle against Finn, king of the Frisians.[2] An ingenious theory[3] has been put forward to explain this Hengist's movements subsequently to the death of his leader, as he is next found, for a time at least, hand-in-glove with the ruler against whom he had previously been fighting. It is suggested that, being an outlaw from Denmark, he remained in Friesland and eventually became the leader of the band of emigrants who settled in Kent.

It is noteworthy that somewhat close relations (*see* the Finn saga) had evidently existed for a considerable time between Denmark and Friesland, and this would serve in some measure to explain the discovery of objects which seem to corroborate this semi-historical tradition. The large number of cruciform brooches which have been excavated from the 'terpen' round Leeuwarden, particularly that of Hoogebeintum, belong mainly to advanced or large types, such as are scarce in North Germany; their source therefore must be sought rather in Denmark, the most southerly land in which this development in size is observable.[4] They were found at Hoogebeintum with burials, a fact which further indicates Jutland as a possible source, as there inhumation is the commoner method

[1] Beowulf, ll. 1069-1159, and the Finnsburg fragment.

[2] The Frisians in question may conceivably have been the North Frisians of the Danish peninsula, but against that must be placed the expedition of Hygelac (Chochilaicus) early in the sixth century against the Franks and Frisians who must certainly be West Frisians.

[3] M. G. Clarke, *Side-lights on Teutonic History during the Migration Period*, p. 185. See also J. Clark Hall, *Beowulf*, p. 180.

[4] P. C. J. A. Boeles, op. cit., p. 17, figs. 25-27, and *Het Friesch Museum te Leeuwarden (Catalogus)*, Nos. 260-268.

of burial in this period.[1] The Frisian power at this date
apparently included the whole of Friesland, Drenthe, Over-
ijssel, and Gelderland, so that its southern borders would be
practically, if not actually, contiguous with the northern
borders of the Frankish group, part of whom buried their
dead in the cemeteries round Bonn and Andernach. There
is nothing geographically inconceivable in a band of Ripuarian
Franks moving down the Old Rhine and after joining themselves with a Jutish contingent, descending on the shores of
Kent. There are certain shades of difference between the decoration of the Kentish bottle-vases and those of the Rhineland,
which suggest a local style of ornament, so that the Frankish
participators in the occupation of Kent may have been the
more northerly members of the Rhenish Franks. In that case
it is only necessary to bear in mind the close affinity between
the patois of the lower stretches of the German Rhine and
Dutch, to realize that the variation in the speech of the two
elements in the fifth century need have been but slight.
Certainly, the amount that is known of the Kentish dialect is
not sufficient to absolutely condemn such a hypothesis. Some
such surmise is essential to explain the two variant elements
in the Kentish culture, as illustrated by the finds from early
graves in that country. It does not exclude the possibility
that the leaders of the immigrants may have been Jutes from
Jutland ; the genealogy is certainly not more than that of the
ruling house, and the name which the settlers bore may quite
well have sprung from the traditions surrounding that house.
The few Danish bracteates may have come from the same
source [2] ; such objects can only have been the possessions of
the higher classes, while the other objects of a non-Frankish
character from cemeteries like Bifrons may represent the semi-
Saxon element from Friesland. In this way it is possible to
bring into line with the demands of some philologists the dis-
crepancies observed by Hoops [3] in the nomenclature of trees,

[1] Müller, *Nordische Altertumskunde*, ii. 185.

[2] For an example from Achlum, Friesland, like some from Sarre, see
Boeles, *Het Friesch Museum*, No. 303, figured on Pl. IV.

[3] *Waldbäume und Kulturpflanzen im germanischen Altertum*, Chap. 14.

cereals, and the like, and other objects of daily use which have led him to favour the idea of a temporary settlement on the Lower Rhine as necessary to explain the acquisition of such names as have an original Roman etymology. Thus, too, an explanation can be obtained for the strong Frankish element in the social institutions of Kent,[1] as also for the Celtic system of land-tenure which Meitzen regards as having been derived from districts west of the Weser.[2]

It is questionable whether the archaeological evidence will support the opinion of Bremer [3] that the chief stream of immigration into Britain came from the *littus Saxonicum* which stretched along the north coast of France and West Flanders. The very proximity of Kent to France makes the denial of any influence from the latter quarter impossible, but so far as Kent is concerned such influence is Frankish,[4] and would therefore not belong to the earliest period of settlement, as at that time the Salian Franks were too much occupied with their own conquests in Gaul.

Actual parallels between the Kentish and Frankish cultures may and do occur in Northern France in large numbers. But the permanent occupation of both Kent and Northern France is to all intents contemporary. What is needed, therefore, is a starting-point for the Kentish culture situated further eastwards, and standing in the same relation to Kent as Belgium to Northern France. For the reasons given, the Rhine alone fulfils all these conditions.

Relations between Kent and France belong rather to the latter part of the sixth century, the time of the marital alliance between the ruling houses and the coming of the Gallic missionaries, to whose efforts, in conjunction with their Celtic *confrères*, the lack of material for the study of Anglo-Saxon art in the late seventh and eighth centuries is largely due.

[1] Chadwick, *Origin of the English Nation*, 76 ff.
[2] Meitzen, *Siedelung- und Agrarwesen der West- und Ostgermanen.*
[3] Paul's *Grundriss*, iii. 859 : *Ethnographie der germanischen Stämme.*
[4] Bremer speaks of Saxons.

NOTE ON THE SAXON SHORE

Two theories have been advanced with regard to the significance of the Saxon shore. According to the first it was instituted to defend the shores of Britain against Teutonic piratical raids. The supporters of the second hold that the Saxon shore represents a tract within which settlements of Teutonic immigrants were permitted. So far as archaeology is concerned, there is not the least warrant for the second of these theories. If it were the true one, it is inconceivable that no traces of such settlements should have been found. What would be required would be a series of finds similar to those from Dorchester and the North German cemeteries, such as those of Hanover. No such finds have been made along the line of coast which constituted the Saxon Shore. The few which are known all come from the south bank of the Thames or further inland, and of these only that from Dorchester need belong to a time before the full tide of immigration set in.

INDEX I

GENERAL

INDEX II

CEMETERIES OR BURIAL-PLACES